Computer-Assisted Research

INFORMATION STRATEGIES AND TOOLS FOR JOURNALISTS

By Nora Paul and Kathleen A. Hansen

with Investigative Reporters and Editors, Inc.

Project editor:
Brant Houston, IRE

Copy editing:
Joanna C. Imm

Book design:
Wendy Gray, IRE

One in an ongoing series of beat books and reporting guides by Investigative Reporters and Editors, Inc.

Please direct comments and suggested updates to beatbooks@ire.org

Foreword

It's been eight years since the 4th edition of *Computer-Assisted Research: A Guide to Tapping Online Information* was published. In those years I shifted my focus from the news-gathering end of the reporting process to the packaging and delivery of online news. Part of my interest in changing focus, apart from always having suffered from a short attention span, was my feeling that after 10 years of evangelizing for efficient, effective, and ethical use of online information resources that the battle was won.

Several things have happened in the past year that made me realize that a new edition, even a complete revision, was needed. One was that I heard from professors who were still using the old (and decidedly outdated) guide in their classes. I even got a request to reproduce sections of the guide from a professor in South Africa. I was gratified to think that the basic principles laid out in the book were still valuable but appalled to think about how many of the links cited in the book had died and how many services had merged. It was time to revisit the resources in the guide and make sure they were up to date.

Another thing that happened is a whole array of new Internet resources valuable to reporters came on the scene that simply were not covered in the last edition. Blogs, Wikis, personal networks, and more sophisticated alert and filter services are all new to the Internet in the past eight years and are well worth exploring.

Along with the recognition of these new resources came the need to expand the "The Four Rs of CAJ" by a fifth "R"—Reconnaissance. As the methods by which people can contribute to information on the Internet become more varied, and valuable, the skills of reconnaissance have become more important for journalists. This guide addresses these reconnaissance techniques.

The opportunity to work with my colleague Kathy Hansen on another book project was too good to pass by. She and I collaborated on a revision of the information-gathering textbook she and Jean Ward had published for years. Working on the book, called *Behind the Message: Information Strategies for Communicators* (Allyn & Bacon, 2004), gave me new insights in how to organize and describe the ways Internet resources can be used for journalists. That Kathy was willing to work on the revision with me made tackling the project much more attractive.

The final deciding point came when Brant Houston said that the guide would be a valuable part of IRE's series of guidebooks for journalists. As a long-time admirer of Brant and the work of IRE, the chance to collaborate on this publication clinched the deal.

There have been substantial enough changes to the book that we decided we needed to make it not just a new edition but a new title. That is why this 2007 version of *Computer-Assisted Research* is subtitled *Information Strategies and Tools for Journalists*.

As always, we hope this guide gives you some ideas on how to use the vast resources of the Internet to support your reporting needs. We would love feedback, anecdotes, and your own tips on how to use the Web well.

– Nora Paul

BEFORE WE START

A FEW WORDS ABOUT THE INTERNET

- ### It is essential

In its early days, the Internet was a "take-it-or-leave-it" type of resource. The range of materials was not vast, there were few tools to help you find things in it, and it was hard to tell where the information came from. You still had to get the information you needed through "traditional" means.

That is not true anymore. Most institutional sources—government agencies, associations, corporations—no longer distribute information through paper-based methods. It costs too much. If you want the press release, report, or latest statistics, you have to go to the Web.

Often, if you want to get in contact with people, the best first access is through e-mail. Increasingly, newsworthy events are happening on the Web—the Web contains an important part of the story being covered (fringe group Web sites, blog entries by people who find themselves in the news, fly-by-night operations run through Web sites). Journalists need to make canvassing the Web a step in their backgrounding before reporting.

- ## It is a supplement

While the above is all true, it is also true that the Internet complements the reporting repertoire and should not replace tried and true techniques. Internet resources and tools might give you a great kick start in your reporting, help you locate that expert, or track down that report you need. But it is just that, a kick start. You will still need to interview those experts and qualify the information in that report.

As with public records and court information, you might find a citation to the information you need but you'll need to do "traditional" paper-trail work to get the full story. So, as much of an advocate as we are for the use of Internet-accessible resources in reporting, we're even more advocates for balance. The Internet is not the whole world of information for reporters and it certainly is not a shortcut around good, thorough traditional reporting techniques.

So, in this guide, which sets out to explain the various tools of online research and pitch their use in reporting, there may be a degree of Internet boosterism. But, before we start, we want to say clearly that the Internet is an essential supplement to traditional journalistic techniques, but it is by no means a replacement.

Remember: It is called computer-assisted reporting, not computer-completed reporting.

A FEW WORDS ABOUT COMMERCIAL SERVICES

This guide is different than the previous four editions because the world of online resources is different. The previous guides focused a lot of attention on the commercial services, many of which provided unique resources. But now the Internet (and, more specifically, the World Wide Web) has become the ubiquitous information delivery tool.

Most commercial database services, ones to which you would have dialed out using a modem to a proprietary server in the past, now have a Web version. Because of this, much of the reference in this guide will be to Internet/Web resources. The section on commercial database services (most on the Web) will detail some of the changes that have happened in the marketplace of large data archives and the contents and uses of these types of services in reporting and research. But because changes in these services are ongoing and the pricing options they offer are vast and convoluted, we will not go into much detail about those aspects of the services.

This guide will focus on the tools and resources of the Internet, for the most part, and try to make comparisons between Internet-accessible resources and the "traditional" information services of the past.

A FEW WORDS ABOUT HOW TO APPROACH INTERNET USE

• Think Small/Think Focus

The cliché about the Internet is that it is the world's largest library but all the books are dumped in a huge pile in the middle of the room and there is no catalog. Well, we agree with the image of the huge pile of material, but not the "no catalog" part. One of the problems with the Internet is there are too many catalogs. The search engines, directories, and other catalogs of Web information are so huge in themselves that they are overwhelming. So, our advice is to think small about the Internet. Give yourself a break. Know that you can't know all the resources, so be kind to yourself. There are dozens of search sites; get to know two or three of them. There are thousands of government sites; decide the ones from which you have a consistent need for information and bookmark those.

Analyze your daily reporting tasks, those things you have to do routinely, and find a few resources that can help you do those tasks. If you frequently have to find people, then get to know some of the telephone/address services. If you routinely look for experts to interview, learn where the best directories and services are. If you cover a particular beat and always need articles and background on that topic, discover a few good Web sites with reliable content or directories to Web sites in that area or set up some news alerts to send you newly posted information. If just one type of information is the meat of your reporting (you're the legislative reporter and you need to constantly track legislative changes), then you might have a bookmark list with just one item on it—the state legislative Web site. And then let that be enough for now. Using a very small slice of the Web well is a whole lot better than trying to use it all and feeling frustrated and overwhelmed.

• Be conscientious

The main idea we preach to journalists using the Web is to be very conscientious about what you are looking at and what is actually happening on the Web site you are using.

If you aren't conscientious, you can easily be misled by propaganda disguised as objective information (a medical Web site which is actually a pharmaceutical company's product). If you aren't conscientious, you might end up relying on outdated information that looks fresh (that great page about a country you are researching hasn't been updated since three governmental overthrows ago). If you aren't conscientious, you can draw conclusions that simply aren't true (you don't find any recent examples of something in a database and conclude there haven't *been* any recent examples—but the database hasn't been updated in nine months).

In the section on using search sites, we will go into a great deal of consciousness-raising tips. In the section on "Evaluating Information Online" we will look at how to be conscientious about the Web site you are looking at. It is essential to know how to judge what these Web sites and services are, what they aren't, what they can do, what they can't, how they were created, who made them and why, and how to know if they are the best, most complete, and most reliable route to the information you need.

- **There are no shortcuts**

The only way to get good at using the Internet is to spend time, lots of time, on it. As professor Jane Briggs-Bunting says, "Surf early and often." Don't try and learn the ins and outs of Web research on deadline.

This guide, and the others cited in "For More Information" boxes throughout the book, will give you some clues and tips to use, and traps to avoid while using these resources in your research. But, just as with learning to drive a car, it's only once you've been around the block a few times that you know how to really handle the equipment and navigate the territory. The exercises at the end of each section on a particular Internet resource should give you some practical experience with accessing and using these resources. Take the time to explore. Time you spend now will save you time on deadline later.

A FEW WORDS ABOUT WHAT THE INTERNET IS, AND ISN'T

What the Internet is:

• Amazing

When you have fast access on great equipment to the whole range of Internet resources there is no more dazzling an information utility. The size, scope, diversity, and entertainment value of the information online is unprecedented. It really is amazing.

• Uncontrolled

There are no standards for the look, navigation, quality, or organization of information on the Internet. That is part of the charm and a large part of the frustration. The rule for Internet searching is "Browser beware."

• Easy to use

After years of struggling with Unix commands and the frustrations of FTP (file transfer protocols), current Web browsers have made the Internet's information easy to access and easy to navigate. If you learn to open an address, click on a link, and cycle back through retrieved pages, you've essentially got the skills required to use the World Wide Web.

• Interactive

E-mail "mailto" links, Internet relay chat, and newsgroups are all examples of how the connections between computers on the Internet allow interaction between you and other individuals and groups.

• Multimedia

In the "old days" of the Internet, files of different types (text, sound, images) sat as separate packages that had to be downloaded and viewed. Now, with Flash and other kinds of Web design tools, these different file types are packaged together on a single page.

• Inexpensive to use

Careful shopping can get you monthly Internet access for less than the cost of a pizza and a six-pack. But the emphasis is on "careful shopping." Look over your options very carefully. Most Internet users today subscribe to DSL service through their local phone company or high-speed cable Internet through their local cable company. If you really want to get online, have e-mail access, and be able to browse the resources of the Internet, the cost of entry is not prohibitive compared to the large commercial database services of the past.

What the Internet isn't!

• The repository of all knowledge

If you ever want to drive a news researcher crazy, just tell them everything you need to know can be found on the Internet. While it is a vast "library of libraries" in many senses, it is not the world's collected knowledge. If you think of available information as an ocean, the Internet would represent a vast atoll, increasingly well populated with information. But that other 80% of the ocean is commercial databases, public records and, yes, books, which contain information and sources that are not, and may never be, found through the Internet's Web sites. Also, be aware that only a small percent of the Internet's resources are found on the surface—learn more about the "deep Web," where the vast majority of information lies, in Chapter 3.

• An information superhighway

The image of a superhighway conjures up a seamless ribbon of smooth asphalt, well-marked and patrolled. The Internet is more a series of information relay stations. One computer link passes off your information request to another. Each substation has its own look, rules, and content.

• Easily used

Sure, the Internet is easy to use, but it's not necessarily easily used as an information resource. Knowing where and how to locate quality information, determining the actual source of the information and pinpointing specific facts can be difficult and frustrating. There are ways to ensure the resources become more easily used (develop research Web pages or well-organized bookmarks) but those are time-consuming to compile.

• Cheap to use

Sure, access costs are low, but time is money! Staying focused in your research goal, having good guides for getting to where you need to go, and stopping when you've found your answers will help keep the cost of your time online down.

• Permanent

Have you ever gotten the dreaded "404 Page Not Found" message? Sometimes the Web seems like an Etch-A-Sketch. The content is there on the screen then someone turns it upside down and shakes – and it's gone. We will give you some tips on how to find the "disappeared" content. But remember, if you find something and need to be sure to find it again – back it up!

While we are decidedly Internet enthusiasts, we also think it is important to keep a strong sense of proportion about its use in reporting. We hope this guide helps you to understand and explore the vast reaches of the Internet. The goal is more thorough, engaging, and informative reporting.

Computer-Assisted Research

INFORMATION STRATEGIES AND TOOLS FOR JOURNALISTS

Table of Contents

Chapter 1

The Five Rs of CAJ

Computers have been changing the way journalists do their jobs ever since newspaper newsrooms threw out their typewriters and switched to cold type production systems, and television newsrooms went from tape splicing to digital editing. This change to computer-assisted production quickly and dramatically altered the way news is produced.

Virtually every news organization has expanded their traditional distribution (newsprint, broadcast, or radio) with digital delivery. Online news has forever changed the way news is delivered.

Then there is the impact the computer has had on news-gathering. "Computer-assisted journalism" (CAJ) is the umbrella term for the use of computers in news-gathering. This term can be daunting because so many different aspects of the journalist's job are lumped under it. Often, people hearing the term think immediately of expensive equipment, complicated programs, and sophisticated analyses, used only in long-term investigative projects.

In fact, CAJ can be broken down into five Rs: **Reporting, Research, Reference, Reconnaissance,** and **Rendezvous**. Each of these functions is critical to news-gathering. While it is possible, and still important, to do these journalistic functions without a computer, today's journalist needs to understand, appreciate, and use the computer-based ways to accomplish these tasks.

Here's a quick look at each of these functions, and how the computer assists:

- **Computer-assisted reporting**: Traditional reporting techniques—gathering information through interviews, backgrounding, observing first-hand, working sources, getting tips—generally have involved working with people. The skill sets of computer-assisted reporting refer to translating these journalistic functions to working with records and data. When journalists are doing computer-assisted reporting they use spreadsheet programs to analyze large sets of records and perform calculations, statistical programs to analyze complex datasets, database software to build original collections of records, and mapping software to visually display data in a geographic context. The information revealed from these techniques supplements the tried-and-true reporting methods without which you'd have numbers but no way to put them into context. Just as journalists need skill in interviewing and getting at the significance of the story from people, computer-assisted journalists require skill in "interviewing" data. The data that result from using these computer applications inform the reporting, point to new trends, uncover the hidden story, and provide independent verification of information.

FOR MORE INFORMATION

Books:

Houston, Brant. *Computer-Assisted Reporting: A Practical Guide.* 3rd edition. New York: Bedford/St. Martin's, 2003.

Bruzzese, Len, Brant Houston, and Steve Weinberg. *The Investigative Reporter's Handbook: A Guide to Documents, Databases and Techniques.* New York: Bedford/St. Martin's, 2002.

Reavy, Matthew M. *Introduction to Computer-Assisted Reporting: A Journalist's Guide.* Columbus, OH: McGraw-Hill, 2001.

Websites:

Computer-Assisted Reporting Bibliography
Compiled by the Poynter Institute's Library Director, David Shedden
www.poynter.org/content/content_view.asp?id=1181

CARstat: Statistical Tools for Computer-Assisted Reporting
Produced by Philip Meyer, Stephen Doig, and Barbara Hansen
www.unc.edu/~pmeyer/carstat

National Institute for Computer-Assisted Reporting
www.nicar.org

Computer-Assisted Reporting and FoI
Stephen Lamble's site of resources and links for Australian journalists
http://members.optusnet.com.au/~slamble

CAR Park UK
CAR resources for UK journalists from Alan Rawlinson
www.rawlinson.co.uk/CARpark_UK

A Guide to Computer-Assisted Reporting:
Tips and Tales of Investigative Journalism
By long-time Raleigh News and Observer investigative reporter Pat Stith.
Poynter Online, June 7, 2005
http://poynter.org/content/content_view.asp?id=83144

- **Computer-Assisted Research**: Research, like reporting, involves a special search or investigation. The distinction comes from the sources used by each. Generally, reporting relies on primary sources (firsthand, independent, and original), such as interviews, observation, or self-conducted computer analyses. Research uses secondary sources (made up of elements derived from something else), such as reports, press releases, and articles. Together, reporting and research help form a complete news report. Databases consisting of secondary sources such as reports, articles, and studies can be used in computer-assisted research. The complexity and diversity of information (and disinformation) resources available through the Internet makes this area of computer-assisted journalism both richer and more difficult to navigate.

- **Computer-Assisted Reference**: References are those quick facts, spellings, definitions, and statistics that add color or detail to your reporting. Reference works—dictionaries, encyclopedias, gazetteers, almanacs, and glossaries—available online, provide quick and handy access to these small but important details. Reference tools also help you get to where you need to go (map tools) or provide leads to sources who might be useful to interview (directories and business guides).

- **Computer-Assisted Reconnaissance**: A lot of what happens online is newsworthy. Much of what you need to know, and stay up to date on, is found online. Savvy reporters realize that the alert services, personalized news, and RSS feeds available on the Internet are excellent resources for keeping up on what is happening. These kinds of Internet tools serve as a journalistic radar. Continuous surveillance of the information-scape is an important part of your work.

- **Computer-Assisted Rendezvous**: A "rendezvous" is defined as a place to which people customarily come in numbers. The "virtual communities" of the wired world are electronic rendezvous spots for journalists. The ability to hang out, listen in, seek advice, and tap into other people's networks of sources is one of the most important new journalistic skills. The newer rendezvous sites such as social networking sites and blogs, along with the older discussion lists, newsgroups, forums, and chat rooms, are important digital meeting spaces for journalists to understand and use.

Each of these five aspects of computer-assisted journalism requires different software, skills, and knowledge. Some are easier to learn than others. Some are more expensive than others. Some are more useful for certain types of reporting than others. Some you use at different stages of reporting than others. All are important parts of your work as a journalist.

If you are looking for more detail on the uses of computers for analyzing large datasets, crunching numbers with spreadsheets, and creating original databases, there are some great books and resources about computer-assisted reporting. Those techniques won't be covered in this guide, although we will look at how to locate data and records that can be analyzed using computer-assisted reporting techniques.

If you are looking for an overview of the other four Rs of CAJ (Research, Reference, Reconnaissance, and Rendezvous), this is the guide for you! Read on for information on the use of the computer to find Web sites, reference works, and information tools, and to connect with people who can help you with researching and writing full, accurate, balanced, and interesting news stories.

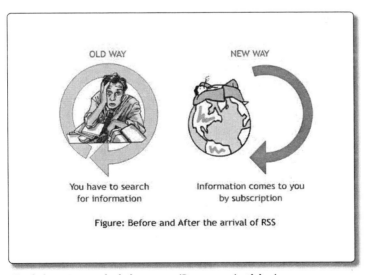

Figure: Before and After the arrival of RSS

Deskshare: www.deskshare.com/Resources/articles/rss.aspx

USES OF ONLINE INFORMATION

Four Stages in the Reporting Process

This overview of the four stages of the reporting process—find story ideas, begin reporting, continue reporting, write the report—outlines some of the computer-assisted research, reference, rendezvous, and reconnaissance techniques and resources to think about using. The following section, *The Answer's Here, What's your Question?*, details specific information tasks and the resources and techniques that can help you get them accomplished.

Find Story Ideas

You need to keep your ear to the ground, find out what the "people in the know" know, and spot trends *as* they are developing. Otherwise, you'll just be following everyone else's leads. Here are some techniques for keeping up with your beat and spotting fresh leads:

• Join a discussion list related to your beat.

• Scan newsgroups on the topic you are covering.

• Monitor alternative sources of information on the Internet, check out zines and niche Web sites.

• Monitor relevant government agency or organization Web sites—check out their "What's New" links or press releases, or sign up for their alert services or RSS feeds.

• Set up a news filter on a topic you want to write about to get the latest news.

• Find a blogger who tracks the topic you are interested in and set up an RSS feed to their postings.

Begin Reporting

You need to get up to speed on the topic you will be reporting on, find background information, do some reconnaissance on the coverage of that topic in other media, and locate people who can give you different perspectives. Try some of these resources to get information, locate sources, and prepare for interviews.

• Check archives of newspaper and magazine articles in commercial database services or through individual news Web site archives.

• Find subject specific Web sites with articles or background material.

• Find "guide" sites which link to good resources for that topic area.

• Post requests to newsgroups looking for people with certain backgrounds or experiences.

• Locate government reports and statistics on government Web sites.

• Locate scholarly articles about the topic, then find the scholars who wrote them.

During Reporting

You need to check the "facts" you get from interviewees, find and qualify the sources you need to interview, and follow up on angles uncovered during reporting. You need to think multimedia: your story will probably be published online; think of the multimedia elements that might help supplement the story you are reporting.

• Use ready reference sources to check spellings, facts, and statistics.

• Use people finders and public records to locate sources and background them.

• Use experts directories from universities and locator services such as Profnet.

• Use government documents to check statistics given by sources.

• Qualify sources' expertise through checks of published material and newsgroup messages.

• Check out multimedia resources: photos, graphics, audio, and video.

During Writing

You need to find "fun facts," quotes and story embellishments to brighten your writing, locate experts who can help interpret what you've found in reporting, and ensure you've kept up with the latest developments in the story you're covering.

• Find quotes and "fun facts" from ready-reference sources.

• Use e-mail to correspond with experts.

• Create sidebars; compile information for graphics; and locate photos, graphics, and art to illustrate the final package.

"Information is the currency of journalism." — John Katzenbach, *Just Cause*

THE ANSWER'S HERE. WHAT'S YOUR QUESTION?

Framing your research strategy

There are different stages in approaching a research task:

- Define the task.

- Frame the question.

- Assess and select the right source for the information you need.

- Select which type of information resource you need.

- Conduct the research.

- Evaluate the results of the search.

This overview provides checklists for thinking at each step.

DEFINE YOUR TASK

Most people think the ability to do good research only requires the right equipment, appropriate software, access to the Internet, and knowledge of how to use the resources. While those are certainly essential to conducting research, they won't get you anywhere but frustrated if you don't approach your research knowing:

- your reporting task,

- the topic on which you are reporting,

- and the type of story you are assigned to write.

In the past, when clip files were the only information resource available in newsrooms (does anyone remember clip files?), the only entry point into researching was by subject (or name or place). But now, with so many types of information resources available through the Internet, some better suited than others for certain kinds of tasks, thinking first about your task will help you identify which type of resource might be most useful.

Once you are clear about the task, you need to frame the question. What specifically you are looking for?

Use the following task inventory to think through your reporting task.

With each new assignment or new day on their beat, reporters and researchers have different information tasks. Look over the following task inventory and think about these breakdowns as you define your own information task. Being specific about your task will help you identify the source for the information you need and select the resource that would be most useful. After each type of specific information task are a few of the tools you might use to accomplish that task.

Reporting task: Locating people

Reporters need people. People tell the stories and bring in the voice, experience, and expertise that takes a news story from a recitation of what happened to a story with context and color. They give an unfiltered perspective and provide a variety of angles on a story. Here are some of the kinds of people-finding tasks journalists have and the resources that might help. Look in the sections on each of these types of resources for more detail about their use.

You want to find a specific person (you know their name). Look in:

- Telephone directories

- E-mail address finders

- Public records databases

- "Google" or other large Web search services

You need to contact people who might know a person who is in the news. Use:

- Neighbors' directories in people finders

- News archives to get names of people who can talk about that person in news accounts

- Blog searches for people who mention the person

You need to interview an expert on a topic you are covering:

- Use expert directories from universities, associations, think tanks, or government staff directories

- Use Google's Scholar search to find authors of reports on the topic

- Post a message to a discussion list on the topic asking for contacts

- Check the newsgroups for people who may have expertise on a topic

You want to identify someone with experience (has had that disease, experienced that event, has been involved in something you are writing about):

- Check newsgroups

- Post a message to a discussion list

- Check past articles in archives for leads

- Contact an association

- Search blogs for people who have written about it

- Find personal Web pages through Web rings

Reporting task: Finding documents

Documents give the background and facts about events, decisions, and rulings. They are essential for getting specific details, for qualifying what people said, for seeing what has already been covered. There are a variety of types of documents journalists need and a number of ways to find them.

Speeches from politicians:

- Governmental Web sites

- Personal Web sites of politicians

- Coverage from news stories

Press releases from companies or agencies:

- Company and agency Web sites

- Press release databases

Court decisions:

- Law library collections

- Court Web sites

- News Web sites linked to court documents

- Legal databases

Reports, studies, and theses:

- University Web sites

- Association and corporate Web sites

- Government agency Web sites

- Indexes to scholarly literature

News articles:

- Individual news Web site archives

- Commercial news archive collections

- News aggregators such as Google News or Yahoo News

- Indexes to print and broadcast news content

Reporting Task: Locating specific facts, statistics, and ready references

You need to fact check, verify what someone told you, or find a fun fact or quote to spice up the report. There are some great resources for finding quick reference answers online:

Find statistics on a topic:

- Government agency Web sites

- Association sites

- Almanacs and yearbooks online

Find quotes or sayings:

- Reference collections with quotations books online

- Specialized quotations collections

Look up spellings, dates, specific facts:

- Ready-reference collections online

Calculate/convert distances, measurements, or currencies:

- Ready-reference collections and online calculators

Reporting Task: Getting up to speed on a topic

A great cartoon by Wiley Miller depicts a man at the front of a line of people, throwing a dart with one hand, his other hand over his eyes. He's standing in front of a huge bulletin board with words all over it: politics, economy, car repair, health care, television, aerospace, bioengineering, foreign affairs, country fairs, oil, vinegar, sports, stocks, bondage, oboe, septic tanks, explosives, liposuction, world peace. The bulletin board says "Today I am an expert in…" The cartoon is titled: "How Reporters Start Their Day at Work."

This sums up well what most reporters and researchers deal with. You don't know what is going to be thrown at you when you get to work in the morning. Here are some of the backgrounding tasks you might have and where to find information:

Background on a country or place:

- Online gazetteers

- Government sites with profiles

- Tourist sites

Background on a person:

- Reference collections and special biography resources

- Newspaper/magazine articles on the person

- Web sites by or about the person

Background on a topic:

- FAQs (frequently asked questions) from a newsgroup on the topic

- News articles

- Web site on the topic

- Association Web site

- Scholarly articles

Background on a news story:

- Current news coverage and past articles

- Discussion on newsgroups and blogs

Angles/slants on a topic:

- Discussion on newsgroups and blogs

Associations/groups interested in a topic:

- Online news coverage

Reporting Task: Staying up on your beat

Staying current and fresh on your beat, getting leads on stories, and tracking trends before they hit the mainstream consciousness are some of the big information tasks of the journalist. Here are some online sources for completing those tasks:

Find out the latest news:

- Set up a news filter to catch articles and blog entries

- Set up a message filter to find who is talking about what

- Check out zines or special publications on the Web

Get story leads:

- Monitor newsgroups and blogs

- Join a discussion list

Create your contacts/sources list:

- Find leading experts through directories

- Monitor newsgroups and blogs

- Read discussion list messages

FRAME YOUR QUESTION

The standard reporting heuristic of "who, what, when, where, why, and how" can also be used to think through the specifics of the research question you want to answer. Having clarity about the questions will help you to recognize when you have gotten appropriate and complete answers—and help you know when you can stop researching.

Get some ideas about the *who, what, when, where, why, how* details you might consider in framing your question with this checklist.

WHO

- **Who is the research about?** A politician, a businessperson, a scientist, a criminal? Knowing this will help you pinpoint the type of resource to use (a business, a government directory, news stories, public records).

- **Who is key to the topic you are researching?** Are there any recognized experts or spokespersons you should know about? Reflect on what you already know about the topic and people you know who are knowledgeable about it. This can help with specific leads.

- **Who do you need to talk to?** Someone who has experienced something, someone who knows someone, someone who has studied something? Knowing what type of people you need to locate can help you pinpoint the resource needed to locate them.

- **Who have you already talked to?** Who do they know? Remember to tap into the sources of the sources you've used—ask whom they would talk to if they had a question.

- **Who has done research on the topic?** Can you find someone who might give you insight into the important questions or angles you should be covering? Find other researchers/reporters/groups who have covered this topic and see what they asked.

WHAT

- **What kind of information do you need?** Statistics, sources, background? Again, this is a task clarification question to keep in mind as you frame your research.

- **What kind of story are you writing?** An in-depth analysis, a backgrounder, a first-day story, a follow-up? Focusing on the type of story you are writing will help you know how much and what type of information you currently need and will help you select an appropriate resource. If you are on deadline, the technique of posting a question to a newsgroup or discussion list might not be the best—turnaround time may be too long. If you're writing a backgrounder, you'll want to get information from the most credible sources to get the most accurate picture. If you're doing an in-depth analysis, you'll want a variety of views from many different perspectives. Each type of story will require a different type of research tactic.

- **What type of information will be useful?** Full-text articles or reports, specific facts, referrals to a person, public records? Visualize the kind of information that would really scratch your information itch.

- **What are you trying to do?** Confirm a fact you've been given, find someone to interview, get up to speed on a topic, background somebody, narrow a broad topic, fill in a hole in your reporting? Again, keep focused on the goal of the research.

- **What would be the best source of the information?** An association, a government agency, a research center, a company? Think about where you would go for information for your question in the "off-line" world and then focus on that type of source online. (Or, for that matter, go for the information off-line.)

- **What information do you already have?** What do you already know about the topic or person? Don't forget what you've already gathered.

- **What would the ideal answer look like?** Would it be a great quote, a chart with statistics, an article titled "Everything you need to know about…" Envisioning the perfect answer will help you recognize it when you find it!

WHEN

- **When did the event being researched take place?** This will help determine which source has resources dating back far enough. Remember that the world of Internet-accessible information is only 10 years old. If you want things back in time, the Internet or commercial archives may not be the place to go—you may need to find original documents from the organization which created them.

- **When did the event being researched end?** Knowing this will give you a good bookend for your research.

- **When will you know to stop searching?** (When you've answered your question!)

WHERE

- **Where did the event you're researching take place?** The answer to this will obviously help you pinpoint local resources, agencies, or news outlets to check into.

- **Where are you in your reporting?** Just starting (looking for background), in the middle (looking for verification of information found), or towards the end (looking to tie up loose ends)? This, along with knowing what type of story you are doing, will help you stay realistic about the kinds and amounts of information you currently need.

- **Where have you already looked for information?** Keep track of places that have helped you in the past on this kind of research mission. If you bring in someone to help with the research, you want to be able to let them know what you've already done and found.

- **Where is the biggest or most relevant collection of the type of information you're looking for?** University research center, association files, specialty database, government agency? Narrow down the hunting ground by thinking through where the type of information you want would be compiled and maintained.

- **Where did the person you're backgrounding come from?**
Determining this, like knowing where the event took place, will help you focus on appropriate local resources and public records.

- **Where might there have been coverage of the event?**
Newspapers, broadcasts, trade publications, court proceedings, discussions, Web sites, blogs?

WHY

- **Why do you need the research?** Reality-checking a source, looking for a source to talk to, surveying a broad topic, pinpointing a fact? Again, clarify your research mission.

- **Why must you have the research?** Can't pitch the story idea without it? Can't prove the premise without corroboration? Keep focused on the goal.

HOW

- **How much information do you need?** A few good articles for background, everything in existence on the topic, just a specific fact? Answering this critical question will help you know when to stop and will keep you on task.

- **How are you going to use the information?** Provide an anecdote to prove a point, illustrate a story statistically, offer quotes to provide voice? Knowing this will also help you know how to attribute and use the information in your story.

- **How far back do you need the information?** Most current year, back 10 years? Keep the range of time you are covering clear. You may select a different source and research technique if you are going back in time than if you just want the most current information.

ASSESS THE SOURCES

Thank heavens we have gotten past the days when people would cite "the Internet" as the source of some piece of information in their news story. Information online does not just come out of some magical combustion between electrons and letters—someone is responsible for writing, uploading, or designing the information found online.

In a textbook on research, *Behind the Message: Information Strategies for Communicators,* the authors (actually, yours truly, Nora Paul and Kathleen Hansen) group the sources of information found online into four categories:

Informal sources: individuals contributing information because of a personal interest, viewpoint, or experience.

Institutional sources: associations, government agencies, businesses, political parties, unions, advocacy groups, foundations, and other organizations which provide information about their projects, business line, or area of activity and advocacy.

Scholarly sources: research, papers, institutes and other resources sponsored and conducted by university and college faculty and students.

Journalistic sources: news reports, series, investigations, and other information reported on and produced by news organizations.

Think about who is most likely to have produced and distributed the kind of information that will answer the questions you have framed or the reporting task you are faced with. Understand why these sources are making the information available and how they have come to know the information they are providing—this will help you in assessing the information from these sources.

INFORMAL

Who they are: People with hobbies, opinions, and experiences (travel, health, life).

Where they are: Personal homepages, newsgroup and listserv postings, blog entries. Informal sources also provide information and reports through journalistic outlets—these "citizen reporters" can provide interesting personal insights into news and events.

How they know what they know: Through their life experiences, their hobbies and interests, their readings, their belief systems.

Why they make the information available: They provide information to share what they know with others interested in the topic or who might get needed support from their experiences. The impulse is about sharing, and, in some cases, demonstrating their own expertise or airing their strongly held opinions.

How you can use this information: To look for people who have been through a certain type of experience (medical, social), to find additional sources with information on esoteric topics or interests, or to locate people who might be connected with other people that would be interesting for you to interview. Following what people are talking about can give you interesting angles on covering a topic.

Cautions: Would you report on what you overhead someone say in the elevator? Using information from informal sources requires the same kind of caution—use the information you read/hear as an interesting launching point for doing the important work of verification and second-sourcing, not as primary source information in a story.

INSTITUTIONAL

Who they are: The people who work for companies, associations, foundations, and government agencies.

Where they are: Corporate, association, government Web sites. They might post messages or provide comments on discussion lists and newsgroups.

How they know what they know: Through the work they do and the responsibilities they have, these sources have gathered information. The information might be generated from specific research conducted in the course of business or might be gathered as part of their responsibility as information stake-holders about the activities of the institution.

Why they make the information available: Information from institutional sources can have a marketing purpose—letting people know about the products, expertise, or research conducted by the organization. Some might be required as part of doing business—financial information in publicly held companies or non-profit organizations. Research and reports from government agencies are part of their responsibility of informing the public which has paid for the research.

How you can use this information: Tapping institutional sources will give you leads to experts on the topic you are researching. The facts and data provided by institutional sources can help you with fact-checking and can provide interesting contextual information.

Cautions: Use the online versions of institutional source information to get an idea of what is available, but be aware that more current information might be available only from the source itself—pick up the phone! Institutional sources can have an agenda. This is not a bad thing, but it is an important thing to be aware of. Knowing the agenda will help you evaluate the context or possible biases of information they have gathered.

SCHOLARLY

Who they are: Professors, researchers, academic institute directors, graduate students.

Where they are: On university Web sites, in discussion lists and newsgroups, in scholarly journal Web sites, in databases of scholarly articles.

How they know what they know: Scholars delve deeply into their field of research and conduct original research, evaluate other researchers' work, and keep current with the latest thinking.

Why they make the information available: Publication of scholarly research is often a requirement for junior faculty, and for all scholars it is a way to share their latest findings and to promote their own expertise in the scholarly community.

How you can use this information: If you need in-depth background or a sense of the scope of an issue, scholarly research can provide it. Scholarly reports also have great links to other material relevant to the topic. The scholars themselves are good interview sources.

Cautions: Sometimes the only way to contact a scholar is through the university information service. They sometimes steer interview requests to the less controversial scholars on campus. Also, scholarly reports have a long publication cycle: be sure to contact the writer of an academic article directly if you want the most current information. Academics rarely work 9 a.m.-5 p.m., Monday through Friday—locating a scholar to talk to might not be feasible with a tight deadline.

JOURNALISTIC

Who they are: You and your colleagues—the reporters, editors, researchers, visual journalists, producers, and news directors who put out the news reports.

Where they are: News sites, blogs, discussion lists.

How they know what they know: Through thorough reporting, analysis of information, and interviewing.

Why they make the information available: News and information are the products of journalistic organizations and journalists are the people who create them. Journalistic information has commercial purposes but also important societal purposes: to create an informed and engaged citizenry.

How you can use this information: Journalism has been called the "first draft of history." These sources are where you will go to find out the latest information, to cover and spot trends, to find the people in the news.

Cautions: News reports can be evolving. Be sure, if you are covering a particular journalistic story, to track developments so that your information is as accurate and current as possible. Also, the "first draft" of history is sometimes incomplete or downright incorrect. Check the accuracy of any journalistic source.

SELECT WHICH TYPE OF INFORMATION
RESOURCE YOU NEED

Which archive has articles going furthest back? Which directory is likely to have the kind of person you are looking for? Which search site most reliably indexes the material you want? Once you have defined your information task and topic, these are the kinds of questions to ask in selecting which resource to use.

Use the following resource inventory here to run through the *who, what, when, where, why and how* questions you should ask yourself as you select your resource options.

WHO

• **Who might have the kind of information you're seeking?** Keep in mind your research task: do you need an archive of news stories, a possible source of the latest statistics, credible background information? Then think about who would provide it. You need to know what types of information are available from different types of resources (news archives, government agencies, public records services).

• **Who would have the most current/most retrospective data?** Some database services have more years available for the same publication than others. Some news Web sites have archives of articles, others don't. Some government agencies keep files of reports, some have only current releases. Answering this question might lead you to off-line research.

WHAT

• **What kind of database should you use?** Are you looking for full-text articles, public records, statistics? Different types of information resources make different types of data available.

• **What type of Web resource would help you?** If you are looking for personal comments about something, then check newsgroups, discussion groups, blogs. If you need credentialed information look into databases of edited articles and reports. If you need data and statistics look for data sets within agencies that compile that kind of information.

- **What services are available to you?** Obviously, this is critical to selecting your access options. This is particularly important when talking about commercial database services available through the Web.

- **What do each of the services offer?** Become familiar with the range of materials each service offers.

WHEN

- **When are the services available?** You can't use an information service if it isn't available when you need it.

- **When should you use another service?** Checking in one resource first (the cheaper or easier one) but not getting anything might lead you to checking in another service.

WHERE

- **Where are you most comfortable searching?** Which service are you most familiar with and knowledgeable about? This is particularly relevant when talking about Web search services—which of the search sites are you most savvy about so your searching can be efficient and effective?

- **Where can you get the best search support?** If your commercial service has a help line and you can get advice on the best search, it may be a better option to use than the cheaper route which makes you muddle through.

WHY

- **Why might you use one service option over another?** Carefully weigh cost, range of material, and ease of use when selecting the search service to use.

HOW

- **How can you make logical selections for which resource to use?** The only answer is to consult an expert (your news researchers) or to develop a wide-ranging knowledge about your access options.

CONDUCT THE RESEARCH

You now know the topic you are researching and what you are trying to accomplish. You've determined the best sources for the kind of information you need and know the type of resource that will most likely contain the information you need.

Now you need to conduct your search. There are some basic questions you should ask yourself as you start to do your research using the resource you've selected. Use the following research inventory to cover those *who, what, when, where, why, how* questions you may have as you jump in and search.

WHO

- **Who can help if you get into trouble during the search?** Be sure to have the help desk numbers handy for commercial services or know where to find the "help" file on a Web site you are using.

- **Who is the expert on searching in your newsroom?** Be familiar with your newsroom's research staff and their expertise.

- **Who can help you put a search strategy together?** You might want to ask the advice of others who have covered similar types of stories. Again, tap into the research expertise of newsroom researchers or locate other journalists who have covered stories like the one you are reporting on.

- **Who are you searching for?** Do you have the correct spelling of their name, and have you taken care to cover possible nicknames or variations? What do you know about them to help you confirm you have the right person in the search results?

WHAT

- **What kind of search will it be?** Is the database resource you are searching a full-text search that looks for words anywhere in an article? Is it a structured public records search where you must use specific types of terms and fields to retrieve information?

- **What search terms will you use?** Work up a list of terms that would be relevant to your search and be prepared to try searches in different combinations.

- **What will you do if you don't find any information (or too much)?** First thing, if you are using a commercial service which charges for the time you are online is to *get off-line* and regroup. In fact, this is good advice even if you are using a flat-rate or free service. You'll just waste time and get frustrated if you don't step back and re-think your strategy.

- **What are the search commands you need to use?** Make sure you are familiar with the search "engine" you are using. Understand the ways to state relationships between the search terms (*and, or, not*), understand how (or if) you can narrow the results, designate how results are displayed. The first stop at any search site should be the help file and the next step in your research is to read it. Take time to learn how to operate the search engine so it can drive you to what you need.

WHEN

- **When should you stop researching? (part 1)** When your search results are totally unexpected—getting too much or too little material, or totally irrelevant material—you may need to re-design your search or take some time to learn how to use the search engine more effectively.

- **When should you stop researching? (part 2)** When your question has been satisfactorily answered or you've found the amount of information you need or can currently deal with!

WHERE

- **Where should you do your search?** Within commercial services, know the range of the data in the variety of databases available, this will help in the selection of which database to use. On Web searches, choose the site that you are most comfortable with or the one that specializes in the type of topic you are covering.

WHY

- **Why are you doing the search?** Keep in mind why you are searching, staying focused on the research goal.

- **Why are you doing the search?** If you are the researcher, should this search be done by the end-user? If you are the end-user, should you have a research expert helping you with the research? (Much of this depends on the resource being used or the complexity of the research task.)

HOW

- **How do you build a search strategy?** Be sure you understand how to link terms within the search (*and, or, not*).

- **How much is the search going to cost?** Know the cost structure of the service you are going to use; this can help you know when to abort a search. Also, think in terms of the cost of time—are you doing not just the most effective, but the most economical, searching.

- **How might you find it cheaper?** Be sensitive to the cost vs. return in your searching. If you just want a few background articles on a news topic that happened recently, find the news sites with free archives for the past few weeks before going online and paying for an article.

- **How will you attribute the information you locate in an online search?** Know the guidelines for attributing different sources. *Never* say "according to the Internet"!

**"Computers are useless,
they can only give you answers."
— Pablo Picasso**

Chapter 2

A Conceptual View of the Internet

The computer is the critical tool in the journalist's toolbox.
The computer, essential for writing the story, is also communication central (where internal and external correspondence takes place) and the access point to valuable information resources.

While journalists' comfort with and access to computers has risen in newsrooms over the past decade, there is still a surprising lack of clarity about the component pieces of the Internet, how they can be used in reporting, how they can be used wisely and well, and how you can avoid misusing them. Sure, everyone may be e-mailing, but are they taking advantage of discussion lists? They might be using the World Wide Web, but do they know about the deep Web? They can do a Google search but can they narrow it to find information from a specific top-level domain?

As new types of resources appear on the scene (recent ones include blogs, wikis, podcasts, and social networking sites) do reporters think about how these might be incorporated into their daily journalistic work?

In this chapter we will provide a conceptual view of the Internet—what the pieces of the Internet are and how they fit together. In the following chapters we will look at the different component pieces and examine, in detail, when, why, how, and how not to use them.

The Internet is called a "network of networks." Think of it like the telephone system. If you have an account with a telephone company you can tap into its network of telephone lines and make calls to anyone in the world who is also connected to the telephone lines. In the same way, you can tap into the Internet, this network of networks, if you get an account with a company that lets you access their connection between computer networks around the world.

This connection between computer networks might be through twisted wire cable, fiber-optic cable, satellite, or any combination.

Like the telephone system, each station on this network of networks has a separate identification number, called an IP (Internet Protocol) address. This set of numbers identifies the specific computer network and allows computers to "call up" a specific computer on the network.

OK, folks, that's about as technical as we're going to get with the Internet. If you want to read the whole history of its development and get into the nuts and bolts of its operation, there are some great guides. However, our focus is on what you can do because of this network of networks.

There is a whole suite of information distribution and communication tools developed to be used through the Internet. They can be roughly divided into tools that help you connect to people—primary unfiltered information and conversation—and tools which help you connect to documents—secondary filtered, edited information.

PEOPLE TOOLS

For primary sources: unfiltered comments, discussion, opinion

- **E-mail** (electronic mail): one-to-one message exchange

- **Discussion lists** (aka listservs): one-to-many, many-to-one message exchange through e-mail distribution lists

- **Newsgroups** (aka Usenet): publicly posted messages, like a bulletin board

- **Forums**: newsgroup type areas found on Web sites

- **Chatrooms**: "real-time" messaging where you see the message as it is posted

- **Blogs**: reverse chronological order entries on a personal page of commentary and links of interest

- **Web pages**: personal pages created by individuals on·topics of interest

- **Social networks**: virtual gathering places

DOCUMENT TOOLS

For secondary sources: articles, reports, studies

- **WWW** (World Wide Web): the hypertext document space that is the heart of Internet content

- **FTP** (File Transfer Protocol): an early method used to transfer a specific document from one computer to another, mostly superseded by the World Wide Web. This is rarely used now and won't be discussed in this guide.

- **Telnet**: a technique that used to be required to log into a remote computer and which won't be discussed in this guide

- **Gopher**: an early index of the documents located in Internet networked computers. This, too, has been superseded by the Web and won't be discussed here.

- **News filters**: customizable filters which snag and send information items of interest—usually found as part of a Web site's service

- **Alert services**: subscriptions to Web site updates which are sent directly to your e-mail

- **RSS**: manages feeds of updates from blogs

- **Wikis**: collaboratively written pages which can be edited on the fly

For most people, when they say "the Internet" they mean the World Wide Web. In lots of ways, the Web has wrapped the various tools of the Internet into its information space. But it is important to understand the differences between these information and communication tools and to appreciate how they can serve various uses in your reporting and researching tasks.

So, without further ado, let's look at each of these Internet tools.

FOR MORE INFORMATION

Web sites:

Journalism.net
Julian Sher's site of tips and links for Internet
use in investigative reporting.
www.journalismnet.com

Books:

Levine, John R., Carol Baroudi, and Margaret Levine Young. *The Internet for Dummies*, 9th edition. Boston, MA: IDG Books Worldwide, 2003.

Gralla, Preston, Mina Reimer and Stephen Adams. *How the Internet Works*, 7th edition. Indianapolis, IN: Que Education and Training, 2003.

E-MAIL

E-mail (electronic mail) is the common denominator of Internet access. If you have a way to get on and use the resources of the Internet, you can have an e-mail address. And if you have an e-mail address, you have the means to connect with other Internet users around the world.

E-mail in reporting and research

- E-mail allows you to send personal messages to individuals. You might post a message publicly to a newsgroup, get some responses and then carry on the conversation through e-mail, providing more privacy in the correspondence. Many reporters request that responses to a publicly posted message be sent only to their private e-mail address.

- E-mail can be a more efficient way to communicate with hard-to-reach individuals. Avoid phone tag or rambling voice mail messages by sending someone an e-mail request for information. They can then answer, at length, at their convenience by posting a message back to you.

- Finding an e-mail address might be the only means of reaching someone with an unlisted phone number.

- E-mail can be sent after office hours, and there is a chance that the person you are trying to contact might check e-mail while away from the office.

- E-mail responses put an answer into text form, making it easy (with their knowledge and permission) to incorporate someone's comments into your story.

- E-mail is the means through which you can subscribe to discussion lists.

- E-mail is used to get alert and filter service results sent directly to you.

- E-mail directories can help you find sources that you might not locate otherwise. Some provide profiles that individuals fill out about themselves and they can be searched to find people with particular hobbies or who live or work in specific places. However, no definitive, all-encompassing e-mail directory exists.

- E-mail attachments of photos, documents, and data can be a quick way of getting information from agencies and offices.

What you need to use e-mail

E-mailing requires an e-mail program and an assigned e-mail address.

E-mail software: There are any number of e-mail software packages available and most commercial search sites allow people to create e-mail accounts (e.g. Google's gmail or Yahoo! mail) so it is possible to have a company e-mail address to use for official business, and a personal e-mail address through a Web site where you can do personal messaging. Many people set up an extra e-mail account to use for sites requiring sign-up—these act as "spam" mail drops and keep your business and personal mailboxes clear of marketing, registration, and other non-personal messages.

E-mail functions: Whether you use a software package on your network or through a Web site, the functions of e-mail are basically the same. You receive messages into your inbox. You can display, reply to, forward, or delete messages. You can compose new messages or store messages in personal folders. Some software even allows for pretty sophisticated sorting so that messages coming from a particular discussion list, for example, are automatically sorted and put into a special folder. You can attach files (text, images, datasets) to e-mail messages. Attached files are the way many writers submit stories to publications. The software also maintains for you an address book of e-mail addresses you've used. Each of the functions works a little differently depending on the software package you are using.

The e-mail address: An e-mail address, like a postal address, directs the mail handlers passing e-mail messages through the network of computers to get the message to the right mail slot. An e-mail address consists of four parts. As an example, we'll break down Nora'a e-mail address:

npaul@umn.edu

npaul: Nora's user name. Many organizations have standard formats for user names: first initial and last name or first name.(period)last name. This can be a good way to guess at a person's e-mail address. On non-corporate e-mail services you usually make up your own user name; however, some systems generate random user names. Some services have so many users you might have to choose a very unusual name because all the normal ones you would use are already in use.

@: "at," the universal separator between the user name and the rest of the address

umn: the host computer, the computer where Nora's e-mail box is housed

edu: indicates the type of host computer: edu for university, org for organization, gov for government, com for commercial, net for network—some may have two letters which indicates which country it comes from.

The "umn.edu" is also referred to as the "domain"—the Internet's name for a particular network or computer system. This name is a translation of the actual numerical IP (Internet Protocol) address which, like a telephone number, identifies a specific host on the Internet network. One of the University of Minnesota's actual IP addresses is 128.101.255.255. (IP addresses are always four sets of numbers, between 0 and 255, separated by periods.)

Since numbers are harder to remember than words, these numerical IP addresses are mapped to the domain name. Numeric IP addresses can be found at Whois—the IP address directory maintained by the American Registry of Internet Numbers (*www.arin.net*).

TIPS AND TRAPS WHEN USING E-MAIL

Verification

When telephones first started being used in newsrooms many years ago, the old-timers probably said, "How can you believe you're really talking to the person they say they are? You can't see them!" A similar healthy skepticism is being voiced about using e-mail as a way to contact and interview people. Ira Chinoy, a professor at the University of Maryland, put together a few simple but important guidelines for reading and sending e-mail messages that will be used in stories:

Verify

Just because e-mail arrives with the name of a sender, there is always the possibility of a hoax. If you plan to quote an e-mail message, contact that person directly to confirm that they are, indeed, the author. (And if you can't, don't use it!)

Verify, part 2

If you got an anonymous call claiming something to be true, you'd check it out. The same rule applies on the Internet.

Verify, part 3

Some e-mail systems are capable of passing along, unwittingly, everything a person typed—even errors the sender thought she was deleting. This is not common, but keep an eye out for it. Check with the sender if you suspect a problem.

The rules of libel, slander and privacy are evolving in this new realm. Be alert.

Wise words from Ira, heed them well.

Also, keep in mind how easy it is for people to quickly create an e-mail identity. The use of free e-mail services and the ability to change user names has spawned the practice of "pranksters" who post messages under the name of someone who has just found themselves in the news spotlight. More than one news organization got fooled by the Timothy McVeigh messages on AOL after he was named as a suspect in the Oklahoma City bombing—"the mad bomber" listed under McVeigh's name was not him—as too many breathless reporters had claimed. Verify, verify, verify.

Netiquette

Netiquette, proper Internet etiquette, keeps the unruly world of the Internet a bit friendlier. Bill Ruberry, the Training and Technology Director at the Richmond Times-Dispatch, compiled this list of netiquette tips for e-mail:

- Treat the writing of electronic mail the same as writing a letter on company stationery.

- Check your e-mail regularly and respond to messages within a reasonable time.

- Be careful with humor and avoid sarcasm. Electronic communications can be misunderstood because they lack the voice inflections, gestures, and other body language of face-to-face conversations. A smiley face :-) (look sideways) does not always remedy bruised sensibilities.

- Do not send heated messages, or "flames." Let flaming be a one-way street.

- Don't use all capital letters on your messages. THIS IS INTERPRETED AS SHOUTING.

- Include a short signature file on your messages with your name, e-mail address, etc.

- Include brief, clear, and meaningful titles on your messages so the receiver can have a hint about the contents.

- Never forward personal e-mail to mailing lists or Usenet (or to anyone else) without the author's permission.

- Copy some of the original message sent to you so your response will have a context. Use the > to indicate the part of the message which is being repeated (this is automatic in some e-mail software). But you don't have to send back the whole message which was sent to you.

Most important, remember that e-mail is not totally private and that anything you say on e-mail might end up in the wrong hands, so always consider carefully what you've typed before you hit that "send" key.

Remember, too, that e-mail, like reporters' notes, is increasingly being used as evidence in lawsuits. Many companies are requiring that journalists delete their e-mail to avoid that possibility.

Check your company's e-mail policy to make sure you are using this tool on their time the way they have outlined its use. If your company does not have an e-mail policy, they need to consider one. Take a look at this sample policy from the Associated Press: *http://powerreporting.com/rules.html.*

Spam

Spam messages, the junkmail of the Internet, are the bane of many e-mailers. Generally speaking, they are unsolicited, widely broadcast messages often about a product or service—usually sex related—that you aren't particularly interested in. These unsolicited messages should just be deleted. Don't write them to say "Don't ever send me a message again!" All you are doing is confirming that someone is answering at that e-mail address. So, do what you do with that tire sale flyer or catalog of spiffy golf clothes—throw it out. Be particularly aware of messages that look like they are official business coming from official sources (a bank or online service you use). "Phishers" use official looking communications to try to get people to send account or password information. Remember, most credible sources won't ask you to give them personal information through e-mail.

E-mail hoaxes and viruses

Nary a day goes by without some kind of story about a current e-mail-carried virus. At least once a week we get the latest e-mail hoax ("I am the widow of a billionaire in Zaire and I need help transferring $120,000,000"). When you see these things that look too bad or too good to be true, be a reporter! Check it out. One of the best clearinghouses of various hoaxes and real and pretend viruses on the Internet is found in the Urban Legends and Folklore section of About.com: *http://urbanlegends.about.com.* Snopes (*www.snopes.com*) is another good source. Yet another good source for when these inevitably crop up is Computer Virus Myths: *www.vmyths.com.*

Take care when responding to discussion groups

Remember, if a message is sent from a discussion list, your reply will go back to everyone on the list! Be careful. If you really mean to reply to just one person or think that you are replying to just the person who posted the message, you could really embarrass yourself.

Finding e-mail addresses

There are a number of different e-mail directories on the Web. As we'll be discussing in the section on "people finding," you'll learn with e-mail directories that the best one to use is, well, the one which has the person you are looking for in it. That might require some shopping around.

For researchers, the frustrating things about using these directories are not having a clear idea of where the information in the directory comes from, how often it is updated, or just what the scope of the information is. There is such a variety of services, some with different special features, that the best approach is to keep a good handy list of services or use one of the sites which compiles a number of different services on one page and then just flip through them until, hopefully, you find what you need.

Basically, e-mail directories let you look up a person's name and sometimes designate a particular domain to look for it in. Some do only literal matches of the name, others might find "sounds-like" matches, too. The trouble is, with a common name, there may be a lot of "hits" found—you'll need some other clue to know if you found the right person.

General e-mail directories (primarily U.S. addresses)

For the most part, e-mail directories are pretty useless. In the past few years those sites that had purported to be e-mail look-ups have either disappeared or have discontinued that part of their service. Guessing might still be the best way to find an e-mail address or you might "google" a name to see if the person has written anything that has their address on it.

Here are a couple of sites you can try, but checking several names for e-mail addresses yielded very little information.

- **Infospace E-mail Search:** *www.infospace.com*
  There are directories for international e-mail, too. This found Nora's e-mail address, but from 7 years ago.

- **Yahoo! People Search:** *http://people.yahoo.com*
  There is an e-mail lookup function, but we didn't find anyone we were looking for.

- **Many countries have individual e-mail directories**. One technique for finding them is to use a search engine and search for "e-mail directory" and the name of the country.

Specific e-mail directories

If you are looking for the e-mail address of a particular person or would like to contact someone from a specific company, university, or agency, look for individual e-mail directories or sections on a Web site with a list of e-mail contacts. If you know, for example, the person you are looking for was a graduate of a particular college, see if there is an alumni e-mail directory on the college site. If the person you want is a government official, use one of the government e-mail directories (like the Congressional E-Mail Directory at *www.webslingerz.com/ jhoffman/congress-email.html*) or look at that agency's or branch's Web site.

Free e-mail services

In the growing trend to be all things to all net-users, many Web sites offer free e-mail services. These can be useful if you frequently travel and can get Internet access but have trouble getting behind your company's computer firewall to get your office e-mail.

They are also a good idea because you can have your office e-mail for official business and a free e-mail account for personal correspondence.

The only trouble with some of these free services is coming up with a user name that hasn't already been used! Try a combination of your regular username and a series of numbers.

Another problem with some free e-mail services is that you get spammed. We dropped our Hotmail accounts for that reason.

Here are some free e-mail services on the Web. But there are more available every day:

- **Yahoo!:** *http://mail.yahoo.com*
  Yahoo, the first directory of the Web and now one of the most wide-ranging portals, offers this free e-mail with lots of features.

- **Gmail:** *http://gmail.google.com*
  Google's mail service provides huge amounts of storage space and the ease of Google search for your e-mail messages.

Exercises

- Check the general e-mail directories listed above and see where, or if, your e-mail address is listed. (Now, go ahead and try to find that old boyfriend or girlfriend, no one's looking.)

- There's a new tuition hike at Harvard University that will make it the most expensive school in the world. Find the e-mail addresses of some Harvard students you could contact for comment.

- Find an e-mail directory for Poland.

- Find the e-mail address for a senator from Florida.

- You get an e-mail message with "FW: Fwd: Virus Warning" in the subject line. The message warns you not to open or even look at e-mail that says "Returned or unable to deliver" because it contains a virus. It urges you to pass this warning on your friends. What do you do?

- Try signing up for one of the Web's free e-mail accounts.

"You've got mail!"
— AOL message

FOR MORE INFORMATION

Web sites:

Beginner's Guide to Effective E-Mail
Tips about using a good format, the right tone, and the proper use of greetings and signature files (your identification notice).
www.Webfoot.com/advice/e-mail.top.html

An Introduction to Trouble-Shooting E-mail
Nice intro to all things e-mail,
including how to interpret those "fatal error" messages.
www.maawg.org/khelp/kmlm/user_help/html/troubleshooting_intro.html

Netiquette
Learn the proper manners for e-mail correspondence.
www.albion.com/netiquette

Garrison, Bruce. "The Use of Electronic Mail as a Newsgathering Resource."
http://com.miami.edu/car/miamibeach2.pdf

Books:

Cavanagh, Christina. *Managing Your E-Mail: Thinking Outside the Inbox.*
Hoboken, NJ: John Wiley & Sons, 2003.

Duncan, Peggy. *Conquer Email Overload with Better Habits, Etiquette, and Outlook Tips and Tricks.* Atlanta, GA: PSC Press, 2004.

DISCUSSION LISTS

Discussion lists (aka mailing lists and listservs) along with newsgroups are two ways to join into discussion with other people interested in a particular topic. While newsgroups are modeled after bulletin board message areas, discussion lists are an e-mail routing list. Discussion list software manages the subscription list of those who want to be part of a discussion. When anyone sends a message to the discussion list, the software sees that a copy is routed to all the members of the discussion list.

Discussion lists can be open (anyone who wants can subscribe), or closed (you must prove you have the necessary credentials, usually job position or membership in an organization, to belong). Some discussion lists are set up just for members of a committee to correspond, for people from the same organization, or for students taking a particular class.

There are two types of discussion lists: "Moderated" discussion lists generally have a person who reviews messages posted to the list, ensuring that messages are on topic for that particular discussion list's interests. "Unmoderated" discussion lists just pass along anything sent, sometimes resulting in a lot of "noise" (irrelevant messages) on the discussion list.

Another difference between discussion lists and newsgroups is that a newsgroup's membership is more transient, while the discussion list community is fairly constant. Discussion lists are more for personal/professional support and updating while a newsgroups' messages are more for keeping an ear to the ground on a topic or beat. But both are useful resources for finding tips, getting advice, and hearing about angles to stories you are covering that you might not have thought of.

Discussion lists in reporting and research

There are millions of discussion lists dealing from the very specific (Friends of Conjoined Twins) to the very general (Art History Enthusiasts). When scanning for possible discussion lists of interest, start with a general search and scan for the types of specific topics covered. For example, look for discussion lists on the topic "crime" and you'll find one specifically for discussion of the National Crime Survey and another on the more general topic of juvenile delinquency.

The number of discussion lists is growing rapidly because of a number of services that let individuals set up discussion groups. (In the past people had to have access to discussion list software running on a network.) Services such as Yahoo! Groups (*http://groups.yahoo.com*) have millions of discussion groups, everything from individual family lists to Boy Scout troops, to people who want to join together to discuss particular issues. These can be very esoteric and can be good ways to find people who have had certain kinds of experiences or hold "interesting" opinions on topics.

The people who "subscribe" to discussion lists generally are very knowledgeable and/or interested in the topic of the list either because of their profession or their life experiences. Estimates are that fewer than 15% of the subscribers to a list actively post messages, the rest being "lurkers" (they read but rarely respond). However, all of the subscribers, whether just readers or active participants, have their own personal networks of contacts that might be helpful to you. Posting questions (if they haven't already been posted and answered in the past) to the list can tap you into a group of experts and people with experience. Discussion lists are also often the early warning system for events and trends being spotted by a group of people with a great deal of interest in a topic.

Anyone with a specific "beat" (health or education or the environment, for example) should subscribe to at least one professional discussion list on that topic. This is a great way to keep up with what experts are talking about; solicit information, advice, or contacts from them; and to generally tap into a broad expert base.

If you are going to be working on a long-term project or series, joining a discussion list on that topic can help you come up with story angles and ideas.

One of the great journalist resources combines e-mail messaging and discussion lists. Profnet Experts (*http://profnet.prnewswire.com*) is a discussion list set up for college and university public relations staff. You can register on the Profnet site and then fill out a Profnet search query indicating the nature of the expertise you are seeking, type of organization the experts should be in, and how you prefer to receive a response. Profnet posts the query to the Profnet discussion list. The subscribers of the list (the PR staffs of organizations) read these messages requesting contacts and put the journalist in touch with appropriate experts. Profnet also has a searchable database of expert profiles which directs you to specific people that fit your search criteria. For example, a search for "crime" in Venezuela for "leads" gave us Dr. Jennifer McCoy, director of the Americas Program at the Carter Center. Most contact for experts is through the Public Information Officer.

Other uses

- **Keep in touch with colleagues:** There are numerous discussion lists operating for journalists. Whether you are a copy-editor, a news researcher, a computer-assisted reporting specialist, or a photojournalist, there is a special discussion list of your colleagues. Many are associated with an organization which you might have to join to become a member of the list.

- **Request information, raise concerns:** As a professional development tool, these communities are great support groups. Discussion lists you might join because of beat responsibilities can help you stay up on the latest interests and concerns of the members of that discussion list.

- **Receive zines:** Hundreds of specialty publications are distributed only through discussion list subscriptions. Sign up to get the latest issues. Many of the zines are now available on Web sites rather than through e-mail distribution. The E-Text Archives (*www.etext.org*) is a searchable database of articles from zines with alternative viewpoints. The "blog" phenomenon has taken over some of the role that zines used to play, so be sure to check out the section on blogs in this chapter for more information.

- **Alert services:** Many alert services operate as discussion lists. Sign up with various government agency services and get the latest news releases sent to your e-mail inbox. See the section on alert services in this chapter for more information.

How reporters use discussion lists

Freelance reporter Dave Jackson shares some of the ways he uses discussion lists (in response to a message we sent to the IRE-L discussion list).

"I use discussion lists and listservs as a tool for idea generation, as well as information. I also sign up for e-mail lists for topics I have an interest in learning about, and often, as a result, I at least garner additional information for future use. When I intend to do a story as the result of a specific discussion on an e-mail discussion list or listserv, I always contact the people involved in the discussion that I may or intend to quote. That way I can get their permission to use their comments, but also ask follow-up questions to comments they made on the list, or even dig a little further, explaining an idea even further. Using discussion lists or listservs also allows you to become more familiar with issues or topics that others may lack. A few years ago I was a member of a listserv operated by a government agency focused on disaster preparation. Unfortunately, that listserv was killed, at least for members of the public, immediately after 9/11."

Mark Schleifstein, staff writer at the The Times-Picayune, had this to say about his use of listservs:

"Whenever I start a new investigative/interpretive project, I attempt to identify the listservs used by experts in the area I'm looking. For instance, while putting together our series on Formosan termites, I identified a variety of entomology listservs, lurked long enough to find out which ones were useful, and unsubscribed to the ones that weren't. The useful ones helped us identify key researchers into the effects and treatments for Formosans, and every once in a while produced potential anecdotes that we could use. In one instance, University of South Carolina entomologist Cam Lay explained how he kept a colony of termites in a cooler next to his desk and fed them a variety of materials to see how they responded. That piqued my interest and led to a photographic explanation of how quickly termites can eat through a piece of wood. We were able to get an entomologist at Louisiana State University to put a piece of wood in one of their captive termite nests and take pictures of it over five days to show how quickly the termites ate it."

He went on to describe another listserv useful to his work:

> "As an environment reporter, key listservs are SEJ-TALK (shameless plug
> as I'm a board member and list moderator, but true nonetheless) and
> the tipsheets that SEJ sends out on both environmental issues and FOI
> issues of import to environment writers. The SEJ.ORG Web site also is
> a good source for its ejtoday link, which also is sent out as a "listserv"
> called sej-beat, a listing of key enviro stories of the day."

What you need to use discussion lists

As long as you have an Internet e-mail address through any Internet connected
service, you can join a discussion list. Some discussions lists require users to
have particular e-mail account, such as Yahoo! Groups requiring a Yahoo! e-mail
account (but that's free and worth having).

Cost

Most discussion lists are free; a very few request an actual subscription fee to join.

Instructions for using discussion lists

There are two different addresses for discussion lists. One is the **administrative
address**. This is used for all the administrative functions (subscribe, unsubscribe,
hold messages, etc.). For example, to subscribe to the MIDDLE-L listserv for
middle school educators run by the University of Illinois, you would e-mail
listserv@listserv.uiuc.edu.

The other is the actual **discussion list address** of the list you want to join. The
discussion list address for the MIDDLE-L listserv, for example, is middle-l@
listserv.uiuc.edu. Discussion list software, sitting on a computer somewhere,
might be maintaining a number of different discussion lists. Everyone sends
administrative instructions to that software's administrative address and then
specifies which discussion list they want to subscribe to in the message area.
Discussion list addresses look like e-mail addresses and the administrative and
discussion list addresses differ only in the part before the @ sign; the domain
name is the same.

To subscribe to a list

Send an e-mail message to the discussion list's administrative address with one line in the body of the message: "subscribe listname yourname" where *listname* is the name of the list, and *yourname* is your full name (e.g. "subscribe CARR-L Jane Smith"). When your "subscription" goes through, you will usually be sent a message with instructions for posting and unsubscribing from the list. Keep these instructions; they will help you get the most out of your discussion list subscription.

Sending a message to the list

Send messages to the discussion list address, the one with the specific discussion list name before the @ sign. Be very careful not to send administrative instructions to the discussion list address, only send them to the administrative address.

Tips and traps when using discussion lists

- **Flame-prone lists:** Some discussion list groups are, frankly, friendlier than others. "Lurk" for awhile (read messages but don't send messages) to get a feel for the tone of that particular discussion list. Also, always read the directions for how to post to the list and how to unsubscribe. Nothing generates more irate messages than uninformed users. Getting flamed (receiving curt or cutting messages about your posting) can keep you from getting fully involved in the group. Part of being on a list is knowing that list's style.

- **Stay on topic/know what's been discussed:** Other instant sources of flamebait: people who wander off the topic of the list's discussion or who bring up for discussion a topic that has been discussed to death. Check the archives of the discussion list's messages or find the FAQ (frequently asked questions) document to see if topics you want to bring up have already been covered.

- **Consider the source of the message:** One of the benefits of discussion lists over newsgroups is that the user base is more stable. Some discussion lists (closed lists) restrict members to those who have a legitimate interest or knowledge in the topic being discussed. So, although it is often easier to confirm the legitimacy of the members of a list, it is still important to verify anything posted to a list.

- **Don't quote without permission:** Consider e-mail messages the same as you would personal correspondence or telephone conversations. If you are going to quote, let the speaker (poster) know.

- **Don't use on deadline:** Don't expect to post a message to a list (or a newsgroup) and get an immediate response. If you are on deadline, this may not be the technique to try.

- **Identify yourself:** When messages get posted to the list, they look as if they come from the list, not from an individual, so be sure you add your signature to any message so readers can readily identify who sent it.

- **Be generous:** What goes around, comes around. If you've gotten help or advice from people on the list, be sure to be an active participant and help others. The quality of the discussion depends on the individual members.

- **DON'T SHOUT:** A message typed in all caps looks like shouting in the world of discussion lists. Be sure you don't have cap lock on, and try putting an asterisk on either side of the word for emphasis.

- **Re-read before you post:** The ease and quickness of e-mailing messages to lists can sometimes be dangerous. Be sure to look over what you post before you send it—messages live a long time in cyberspace, and you never know just who will be reading them.

- **Beware the over-flowing inbox:** Some discussion lists might generate dozens of messages a day. If you don't monitor your e-mail inbox regularly, you could quickly be overwhelmed with messages. Some discussion lists provide a "digest" feature which merges all the messages sent to the list and sends out just one huge message to your mailbox each day. This can cut down on the message volume.

- **Pick your group carefully:** Make sure the community you are joining is the right one for you. You will be getting lots of e-mail, so if you find that most messages are irrelevant or annoying, it will only be taking up your time.

- **Don't advertise:** Most discussion list subscribers deeply resent being used as a promotions mailing list. Unless the group specifically allows advertising type announcements, don't send them.

- **If it's personal, send it to a person:** Be sure to send messages that might have limited interest to the whole group to specific people rather than to the discussion list.

- **Ask for help if you need it, not just because you're lazy:** Sure, you can post to an astronomy discussion list and ask for an explanation of the "big bang," but you will probably get flamed. If you can look it up, don't expect the members of the discussion list to waste their time responding. And don't send out 25-question surveys to a list—you'll just be ignored.

Bill Ruberry, the Training and Technology Director at the Richmond Times-Dispatch, has these additional tips for effective and safe use of discussion lists.

- Avoid embarrassment by taking care in replying to messages or posts. You could unwittingly send a communication intended for one person to an entire mailing list or newsgroup. Automatic replies typically go back to the address that originated the post—in many cases, a list or group. It's often best to type in the address instead of relying on the "reply" button.

- When publicly replying to a message, summarize the original message or copy enough of it into your response so other readers will understand the context.

- Do not cross-post the same message on many newsgroups or mailing lists unless it is clearly appropriate.

- If you discover an error in your post, correct it as soon as possible.

- If you post a question, be sure to follow up later with a summary of the replies.

- If a message is more than 100 lines long, alert readers by putting the word "Long" in the subject header.

- Avoid "me too" messages. Merely agreeing with a post without offering a new idea is frowned upon.

- Make messages reasonably brief and to the point. Rambling is a no-no.

How to find discussion lists

Maintaining a directory of discussion lists is difficult and the departure of some of the key guides from the past, most compiled by individuals, is evidence. The large information sites have become the hosts for, and catalogers of, many of the operational discussion lists. Here are some ways to locate discussion lists.

- **Yahoo! Groups:** *http://groups.yahoo.com*
  Host of millions of discussion groups, Yahoo!'s directory and search engine make it easy for journalists to find a discussion on almost any topic. Information about each group includes: date founded, number of members, message volume history, and a full description of the goal of the discussion.

- **Tile.net:** *http://tile.net/lists*
  TILE.NET, "The Reference Guide to E-mail Newsletters and Discussion Lists," has indexes to discussion lists grouped by description, name, and domain. There is also a search function that will look for the words you type in the name or description of the list. Information about the discussion list includes how to subscribe to the list.

- **CataList:** *www.lsoft.com/lists/listref.html*
  Lists over 55,000 public listservs. Lists of interest can be found by searching a keyword, by country, and by number of subscribers. Information about the lists found includes: number of subscribers, registration instructions, and list "owner" contact information. Access to archived messages from the discussion group is available.

TILE.NET/LISTS
The Reference Guide To Email Newsletters & Discussion Lists

Email Newsletter - Ezine List Name: JOURNETHICS

Description: Ethics in Journalism forum

To unsubscribe send an email to the **Mailto:** address listed below with the **Unsubscribe Info:** in the subject line.

Unsubscribe Info: unsubscribe JOURNETHICS

To subscribe send an email to the **Mailto:** address listed below with the **Subscribe Info:** in the subject line.

Subscribe Info: subscribe JOURNETHICS

To email the Administrator, substitute the @ sign for **AT** in the below address. This has been put in place to protect the adminstrator from SPAM.

Administrator: owner-JOURNETHICS AT lists.missouri.edu

Mailto: listproc@lists.missouri.edu

You can also find discussion lists of interest by searching in Google or other search sites on "discussion lists" or "listserv" and a topic.

When using directories of discussion lists remember what it is you are searching for. Directory databases contain only a minimum amount of information about each discussion list, name and a brief description and, possibly, some keywords. You are not searching the actual content of the messages posted to the discussion list. So, keep your search general. You'll be more likely to find references to relevant discussion lists than if you get too specific.

Be sure to read the help file on the directory site to do the best search. Some directories, for example, ignore punctuation, so if you look for that great CARR-L discussion list address by typing in CARR-L, it won't be found. Just type CARR or Computer Assisted Reporting.

Some directories have two ways to locate discussion lists: a general search which looks for words anywhere in the entry, and a browsable alphabetical list to look up lists by name.

When you've located a list that looks like it might be interesting, send a message to the list "owner" (the person who either started or maintains the list) to get more information about the kinds of things that are discussed and, if you have concerns, whether or not journalists would be welcome as part of the group.

A quick comparison

We looked for lists discussing bioterrorism issues and found the following:

- **CataList:** Searched for "bioterrorism" in the list name or list title and found eight lists, from the Bioterrorism Portfolio (with 1,835 members) to the Indiana University Medical Group's Bioterrorism list (with two members).

- **Tile.net**: None found in either searching or directory look-up.

- **Yahoo! Groups:** Twenty-two groups found covering topics such as biodefense, the "Cities Readiness Initiative," and the San Diego Bioterrorism and Disaster Defense Council. The Yahoo! search has the most material to search on because of the descriptive entry about the list.

Of the discussion lists found, none were found in more than one directory.

Archives of discussion list messages

It used to be that discussion list messages were accessible only to those who subscribed to the list. Discussion list subscribers could send a command to the list to perform a search of messages sent to the discussion list and any that matched the keywords would be delivered in an e-mail message.

The discussion lists hosted by Yahoo! Groups have the archive of past messages immediately available. Some of the groups require membership to read the past messages, others are open to the public. You can search for messages containing particular words and many of the posters of messages have links to their Yahoo! profiles so you can get a little background about the person who sent the message.

The service "Open Subscriber" (*www.opensubscriber.com*) archives about 2,000 public mailing lists' messages and provides a simple search to locate messages. Discussion lists can add Open Subscriber to their mailing list and then the messages posted to the list are archived and made searchable.

Exercises

- A new treatment for Parkinson's disease has been announced. Find a few messages about Parkinson's disease.

- You've just been named your paper's cops reporter, a new beat for you. Find a discussion list that would have colleagues you should bond with.

- Now, think of your favorite hobby and find a group you'd like to join with that hobby or interest, and go sign on!

NEWSGROUPS AND FORUMS

Using discussion lists is one of several ways you can read or take part in discussions between individuals on the Internet. Another is to join a chat session. And one of the most popular is to join a newsgroup. The main differences between these forums are that you sign up for a discussion list and the messages go to your e-mail inbox, you go into a chatroom and see the conversation in "real-time," while you go to a newsgroup area and read and post messages like on a bulletin board.

Newsgroups are actually the collection of articles distributed through Usenet, a system developed in 1979 at Duke University to pass messages from one network to another (rather than to individuals). The newsgroups are the subject organization of these Usenet messages.

Forums are like newsgroups but they are generally found as a feature within a Web site. An individual Web site will host various forums for its users to allow them to post comments, raise issues, and get group support.

Newsgroup and forum messages are posted publicly, available for anyone to read and respond to.

Newsgroups and forums in reporting and research

- **Story ideas:** While some of the messages will be more like CB radio talk, others can give you a first alert about a developing new topic or area of concern to the group. You can get leads and angles on a story area you are working on. Browsing some newsgroups of interest to see what topics really have people going (lots of messages posted about a particular topic) can be a good tip to a likely interesting story.

- **Finding sources to talk to:** The people who read newsgroup messages are a great source for information themselves, and they know others who are experts or experienced in the topic being discussed. By connecting to a newsgroup's population, you are connecting to their social and professional networks.

- **Seeking people who know about a specific topic:** Again, anyone who joins a newsgroup is likely to be very interested, concerned, or knowledgeable about the topic being discussed. The group is highly motivated to share information and to support the questions raised by other members.

- **Find people it might be hard to find otherwise:** Doing a story on a new arthritis treatment? How would you find people who want to talk about it or who have used the treatment? Go to alt.support.arthritis. People getting support for diseases or personal situations can be located in newsgroups.

- **Get good backgrounders:** Most newsgroups have compiled FAQs (frequently asked questions) for their topic area. These often answer the basic sorts of background questions you might have when you need to get up to speed on a topic. Find FAQs from Usenet newsgroups at Internet FAQ Archives: *www.faqs.org/faqs*.

- **Find key articles and esoteric documents:** Newsgroup members frequently post articles and reports they have found and that they think will interest others. You can sometimes find articles that you might have had to go into a subscription site to get. (Of course, copyright is a whole other issue that we won't get into here.)

- **Your news organization's Web site:** The forums hosted by your news Web site can be valuable resources in your reporting. Check the comments and complaints about news stories that have been covered and you'll often get sources or story ideas.

Newsgroup and forum anecdotes

Freelance reporter Dave Jackson shares his views on the uses of newsgroups:

> "I first found Usenet back in the days when I had a Prodigy account,
> maybe 1988 or 1989. I was surprised that I hadn't heard about it back
> when I was using BBS (Bulletin Board Services), and I thought it was
> great! I became more interested in it just before the fall of the Berlin
> Wall and have used it as a tool ever since. To this day, as I've done in
> the past, I use Usenet to find contacts, sources, and information. Once
> I find an "expert" on Usenet, I get their contact information, verify their
> background and expertise, as I would anyone else, and go from there. If
> they pan out and really are "experts" at what they say, I contact them."

What you need to use newsgroups and forums

Newsgroups are actually just the subject collection of articles distributed through
Usenet. In the past, the network or service you used for Internet access had to
have the Usenet mail reader software loaded, and the newsgroups you wanted
to read had to be "subscribed" to by the software.

But now anyone can get newsgroup message access through Google Groups
(which purchased the old DejaNews service, the previous compiler of Usenet
messages).

Forums are found on individual Web sites so to get access to forums, all you
need is your browser and access to the Web.

Cost

There is no fee for reading newsgroup messages or for joining newsgroup discussions. Some forum areas might be restricted to subscribers of the Web site
if the Web site is one that requires a subscription or registration.

Tips and traps when using newsgroups and forums

Newsgroups and forums are great resources for connecting with experts and people with certain types of experiences. However, there are some things you should keep in mind as you use them:

- **You need lead time:** You might post a message and not get a response for a day or two. Don't rely on responses for short deadline stories.

- **Identify yourself:** Although you're in cyberspace, you need the same ethics as when you're dealing with people face-to-face. If you are trolling for comments to use in a story, be sure to disclose who you are and something about why you are looking for comments.

- **Remember, anyone might read what you post:** Don't tip your hand on a big story, there may be other journalists out there. Be as vague as possible but specific enough to get some response. Ask people to reply to your e-mail address, not to post to the newsgroup.

- **Verify, verify, verify:** Would you put in the paper something you heard at a cocktail party without verifying it? Of course not. Same with what you read in a newsgroup.

- **Read the FAQs:** Don't become instant flamebait by asking a question that has already been answered by the group. Be sure to find and read the FAQ document which most newsgroups have available on their topic.

- **Search the archive:** Many newsgroups retain an archive of messages. Before you send out a question, search to see if it has already been addressed by the group. Google Groups has archived Usenet messages back to 1981.

- **Get a sense of the climate before you get active:** Lurk (read messages but don't send or reply) for awhile on the newsgroup before you become active. Learn about the community of people, their concerns, and their tolerance level before you solicit information from them. Be as sensitive to the group as you would be in a face-to-face situation. And don't overdo it. When Jerry Garcia died, a message was posted by a journalist to the rec.music.gdead newsgroup, asking for stories or memories anyone would like to share, information about local vigils, etc. One member of the newsgroup responded, "You want a comment? How about 'GO THE F*** AWAY!' You can read the posts here. People are upset. Stop digging for news bites and let us grieve!" Bottom line: this is a great resource for journalists, just be sure to use it appropriately and sensitively.

- **Find a few to monitor:** As with all Internet resources, if you start off thinking you have to eat the whole thing, you will quickly have a stomachache. Take small bites, find a few good places, monitor them well, gradually build up your skills, and gradually get this technique for covering your beat incorporated into your style of work.

- **If there is a choice between a moderated and an unmoderated newsgroup on a topic, go moderated:** Moderated lists usually have someone who oversees the message traffic to see that it stays on topic and to mediate flamewars. Unmoderated lists are "anything goes," and what often goes is trivial, off-point kinds of messages. Most newsgroup lists and finders will indicate whether or not a newsgroup is moderated.

- **Remember the audience:** Newsgroups and forums, more than any other tool on the Internet, are the most problematic in terms of verifying the source of information and determining its agenda. Newsgroups provide truly unfiltered information and should be used carefully. Depending on the kind of story you are doing, they can be a great source. When rumors were rampant about an errant military jet pilot who disappeared over Colorado, newsgroups were a great place to go to read the crazy theories for a story on, well, crazy theories. These are the bar rooms, locker rooms, and living rooms of the Internet.

How to find newsgroups and forums

Usenet newsgroups are organized into nine main areas, regulated by Usenet, and hundreds of other areas which anyone can start up. The main nine are:

Alt	Alternative topics
Biz	Business-related topics
Comp	Computer-related topics
Misc	Miscellaneous topics
News	Current events
Rec	Recreation and entertainment
Sci	Science
Soc	Society and culture
Talk	Discussion and debate on many topics

The largest and most wide ranging newsgroup is alt, for alternative. Here's where you will find all the fan newsgroups and bizarre interest areas.

Newsgroup names are a series of letters and words separated by periods, for example, soc. culture. african.

Forums are discussion areas found in various Web sites and by different Internet providers (like AOL). They are often called the Bulletin Board or Feedback. Getting into a forum area often requires a registration (they want to keep track of who has come onto their service). These communities are generally a bit more controlled than newsgroups. If you are looking for people who might be talking about a topic you are interested in, check with the major Web sites for that topic area. Chances are excellent that one or more will have some sort of forum area on the site.

If, for example, you are interested in issues going on in a particular part of the country, going to the local newspaper's Web site and reading the forum area postings might give you some insights (though don't be surprised if the thing people seem to be most agitated about is the local sports team!).

These forum/bulletin board areas are often hidden down in the site, so it can take some looking to find them.

Finding newsgroups and newsgroup messages
on Google Groups

Google Groups (*http://groups.google.com*) has two levels of searching: simple and advanced.

- **Simple search:** Plug in a word in the search box at the top of the homepage. You'll get a display of relevant newsgroups and then a listing of messages containing the word you've searched.

- **Advanced search:** Click on "Advanced Search" and get a search form which lets you type in keywords and designate "and" ("with all of the words"), "or" ("with at least one of these words"), or "not" ("without the words") relationships between them. (See the section in Chapter 3 on searching for more about "Boolean" connectors—*and, or, not.*) You can also search for messages from specific groups, messages where the word you are searching is in the subject line, messages from particular authors (input their e-mail address), messages in a particular language, and messages posted by date.

- **When reading old messages**, be aware that the e-mail addresses of posters might have changed. Fresh messages might be better if what you are looking for is people to contact.

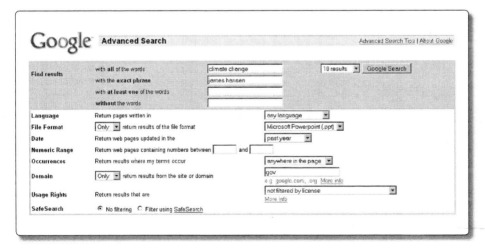

Reading the results page

At the top of the results page, you'll be given the names of (and links to) news-groups where the search term you entered is likely to be discussed. If you want to see recent messages posted, click on the newsgroup name. This is a good technique if you would like to see what people are discussing or to locate a group which might respond to a message from you on a particular subject.

Underneath the newsgroup listing you'll get a list of messages which contain the search term you used. These will come from a variety of newsgroups (some of which were not on the listing of newsgroups at the top of the page).

You'll get a listing of messages in reverse chronological order. This is a good technique if you want to find people who have commented about a topic or would like to browse through messages on a topic to get story angles and ideas.

Categories

Google Groups has a subject directory of newsgroups that can be used to find appropriate groups to browse. There is a separate search box that will just locate groups. Clicking on one of the broad categories listed will get you to a more specific listing of groups by topic (under that broad category), region, language, level of activity, and number of members.

Reading the messages

Once you've located some messages or found a newsgroup there are a few things you can do:

See the "thread": Next to the message is a link that says "view as tree." Clicking on this will show you in the left-hand margin the message thread, the flow of messages on a particular subject displayed like a diagram. If you want to start at the top of the thread, click on Msg 1. Displaying the message "tree" (as Google calls it) will let you move through the messages.

Read the message: Click on the underlined message to get the text. When you pull up a message, click on "show options" to get the following information: author of the message, date it was posted, and the forum it was posted to. In the text of the message you'll sometimes see > or >> marks in front of lines. These indicate they are a copy of lines from a previous message to which the writer is responding. The "RE:" in the subject line of a message indicates the message is a reply to another message.

Message Options: If you click on the "options" link, a variety of possible actions will be displayed:

> **Reply:** Click the "reply" link to pull up a text box where you can type in your message. Some groups require you to be a member. (On Google, becoming a member is simple.) This reply will be posted to the entire newsgroup.

> **Reply to Author:** Click this link to send a message to the person who wrote the message. Only that person will see the comment. This is what you want to do if you are interested in talking with an individual.

> **Forward:** If you would like someone else to read the message (or send a copy to yourself) the "forward" command will pull up an e-mail box.

> **Print:** Print (duh!)

> **Individual Message:** This will change the display of all the messages to show only the one message you are looking at.

> **Show Original:** This will give you the message with all the network routing information.

> **Report Abuse:** This link pulls up a box that allows you to alert Google if a message is spam or contains illegal content.

Author Posting History: You see an intriguing message from someone and might want to contact him or her for an interview. Check out other things the person has posted by clicking on "Find Messages by this Author" (found next to the author's e-mail address). It will give you a listing of the messages the person has posted in various forums. Sometimes just reading the types of forums the person has posted to provides interesting insights into the person and his/her interests.

Sorting Messages: Messages can be displayed by "relevance" or by date. Depending on what you are seeking, one or the other display would be more appropriate.

Exercises

- After another traffic death involving air bags, you are investigating the issue of air bag usage. Find some newsgroup messages to get some ideas of issues people are talking about.

- You're going to be doing a series on domestic violence. Find some forums where this is being discussed.

- You've just gotten a job at the Miami Herald and would like to know about some of the issues that have people talking down there. How would you find that out on a forum?

- A member of your family has been diagnosed with diabetes. Find a support group for them.

FOR MORE INFORMATION

Wikipedia entry on Usenet
http://en.wikipedia.org/wiki/Usenet

Usenet Newsgroups for Journalists
Compiled by San Francisco State University.
www.journalism.sfsu.edu/www/internet/usenet.htm

CHAT

Chat rooms, along with e-mail, discussion lists, newsgroups, and forums, are a way to connect with people and their raw (sometimes very raw), unfiltered opinions and perspectives.

The other people-connection tools are delayed delivery (asynchronous) of the message. For example, e-mail or newsgroup messages get sent and might not be read by anyone for some time.

Chat rooms, on the other hand, are "real-time" conversation (synchronous) conducted in virtual meeting halls. When you enter a chat room, you can see the messages as they are being typed by others in the chat area, and you can type in an immediate response.

We have a bias against chat room discussions—for the most part we think they are incredibly shallow and a waste of time. They are chaotic, it's hard to follow the threads of conversation going on, and it contains usually the lowest common denominator of conversation, with lots of short, pointless comments. But, that is now, and if chat matures as quickly as other aspects of the Web, then this is an Internet tool well worth watching. There is budding potential use for reporters.

Uses of chat in reporting and editing

Chat has become one of the favorite features that Web sites offer to pull in users. Many sites sponsor chats with celebrities or experts. Subject-specific Web sites often have online live discussions with prominent people. These virtual Q&A sessions have an advantage over the live speech because the text of the questions and answers are captured.

Journalists can hold virtual interviews by scheduling a meeting in a chat room with a source and the interview can be held there (again, with the advantage of the text capture). Many find that a chat room interview is more free-flowing than conducting an interview via e-mail.

Chat anecdotes

Freelance reporter Dave Jackson shares this story about using chat technology:

> "I've used a variety of chat tools over the years, having learned an impor-
> tant lesson in the usefulness of chatting and IMs (Instant Messaging) as
> the former Soviet empire was crumbling. I had an AOL account at work
> back in 1991, and while logged in to an AOL chat room, blowing time
> before a deadline, I found out just how handy chat could be for getting
> information quickly. I found someone who knew a friend in Moscow.
> That person used Internet Relay Chat, or IRC, to communicate with
> friends around the world. As a result of the chatting with the Russian,
> who spoke fairly decent English, I was able to get information as it was
> happening. As we went to press, we had more up-to-date news than
> was available on the wires.
>
> I've used chat many times since then to cover other stories and have
> done follow-up to interviews with various government and business
> leaders using IRC or chat tools."

Tips and tricks when using chat

Chatters use lots of shortcuts to speed up their communication and to give
a sense of tone to their words. They often use "smileys" or "emoticons," little
graphics which denote a reaction: smiling, frowning, puzzled, etc. And they
use acronyms: IMHO—in my humble opinion, TTFA—ta ta for now. Decipher
them with these lists:

- **Acronyms used online**: *www.sharpened.net/glossary/acronyms.php*

- **Emoticons**: *www.computeruser.com/resources/dictionary/emoticons.html*

  www.muller-godschalk.com/emoticon.html

What you need to be able to chat

There are three different ways to get into the chat scene.

The original way to chat was using IRC—Internet Relay Chat. You had to download software like mIRC before you could hook up with and chat to other users. There are more than 44,000 different chat "channels" on the IRC.

You can also download various other chat software programs, freeware (no cost) or shareware (low cost), that let you chat with other users of that particular chat software. You can get a good explanation of chat software and links to various versions at Internet Chat Software: *www.softdepia.com/chat_sub_114_1.html.*

Finally, you can join the chat areas, or chat rooms, found on many Web sites and most of the major search services (e.g. *http://messenger.yahoo.com/chat.php*). Some sites specialize in chat only (e.g. *www.talkcity.com*) and host hundreds of different chat areas. These require no other software than just the browser software you use to get on the Web. However, there is often a registration process required before you can get into the chat areas on a Web site, but it is usually free.

Beyond text chat

Internet technology and tools have advanced to the point where we don't rely on just text anymore. Video and audio chat rooms make the chat experience much more personal. If you have a webcam or microphone you can join in audio and video chatrooms. To find out more about the requirements of audio/video chat and to locate some chat rooms where you can be seen and heard go to:

- **Camfrog**: *www.camfrog.com*

- **PalTalk**: *www.paltalk.com*

Videoconferencing and webcasts are increasingly being used by organizations and government agencies to hold informational meetings and training sessions. You can sign up to experience them "real-time" or, often, the webcast will be archived for later viewing.

How to find chat areas or chat events

- **Chatmag**: *www.chatmag.com*

"The Internet's Largest Chat Room Directory." Find chat areas by state and by 350 topic areas.

Exercises

- You're in a chat room and someone types "GAL" in response to a insightful message you sent—should you be insulted?

- You cover health and like to keep an eye out for interesting topics and discussions. See what chat events will be coming up that might be interesting for the health beat.

"Now they're bouncing messages off the stars. Bet the messages aren't worth the technology. Think of 'See you Friday, Ethel,' chattering round the eternal spheres."
— Dick Francis, *In the Frame*

ALERTS, FILTERS, AND RSS FEEDS

Alerts, filters, and RSS feeds are powerful tools of reconnaissance for the journalist. When you are following a particular topic, watching for updates to a specific Web site, or interested in the insights of a certain blogger, these updating utilities can be your best friend. The unending flow into the Web of new information, messages, and news stories can be a tsunami. These resources can help you to identify specific streams of information you want to be kept aware of. They will help you keep your head above water.

The terms "alerts" and "filters" are sometimes used interchangeably. Here is the distinction we make between the two. An alert is a broadcast sent to all of the people who sign up for the alert service. They operate like a listserv in that you sign up to be on the list of people who get sent a message when there is breaking news or if you want a daily listing of headlines—everyone who signs up for the alert will get the same thing. These are usually sent to your e-mail address, although some alert services require a software download which enables the alert to pop up on your computer screen.

A filter, on the other hand, is a customized profile you set up that identifies your topic interests. These are personalized information streams sent to your e-mail inbox. When the filter captures something on the Web site that fits your profile, you will get a link to the item sent to you. You can have a number of different filters going at the same time.

And then there is RSS. RSS (Really Simple Syndication or Rich Site Summary) is increasingly used by Web sites and blogs to allow people interested in getting the latest updates to the sites to "subscribe" and have the latest entries sent to them. RSS feeds require a "reader," a software program which manages your subscriptions and allows you to scan the new entries from the variety of sources you have selected.

Uses of alerts, filters, and RSS in reporting and editing

Reporters covering a beat or working on a longer-term story would be well served by setting up a couple of subject filters to stay fresh on developments, to hear about new facets of the topic you may not have thought of, or to build a resource list of interesting experts. This is also a way to get anecdotes or color pieces that might add interest to your own coverage.

Busy journalists who need to keep abreast of information from a variety of sources or who have favorite commentators or bloggers they like to follow can use RSS feeds as a way to manage the flow in and the scanning of new entries.

Alert, filter, and RSS anecdotes

Freelance reporter Dave Jackson shared this information about his use of RSS feeds:

"I use RSS feeds to keep up-to-date on news, breaking news, and agency- or organization-specific information. I have two RSS feedreaders installed. They are Pluck (*www.feedreader.net*) and Tristana (*www.tristana.org*) as I haven't yet (after more than a year!) decided which one I like best. In Pluck, I have all governmental RSS feeds that I monitor, which makes it handy for keeping things separate. In Tristana, I have all the other RSS feeds, including ones for medicine/health, non-profits, corporate/business, news/breaking news, and politics.

Another tool I've found useful over the years is ChangeDetection.com. It's a service that monitors Web pages, and whenever there's a change to the page, I receive an e-mail alerting me to the change. The only downside to Change-Detection is that the notices are sent once daily. The upside is that I always find out changes made to just the specific pages which I am interested in on specific sites."

Tips and tricks when using alerts, filters, and RSS

Generally, news alerts simply require a quick sign-up to add your e-mail to the list. These are really like signing up for a electronic mailing list but the flow is one-way—they are not for corresponding with others on the list. Filters, on the other hand, require some care when designating the terms you want to use as your filters. Simply putting "Bush" into a filter, for example, will get you newly posted articles about the president, but you'll also likely get gardening tips about shrubbery. Finding that delicate balance between "broad enough to capture what you need" and "narrow enough to get what you really want" can be tricky.

Be sure to look carefully at the service providing the filter. There are sometimes options for how often you get the items captured by the filter. If the updates you want are "mission critical," you might want to choose the option that sends new items to you as soon as they come in. If you are just scanning for a topic, a daily digest of the relevant items might be all you need.

Some alert services are set up to just send alerts directly to your e-mail inbox. Others provide a "desktop" alert service, which will pop up a window on your computer when new alerts are sent out. These generally will require that you download a software program. The BBC's "desktop alert and breaking news service" (*http://news.bbc.co.uk/1/hi/help/3533099.stm*) offers both styles. You have to decide what style best suits you. Do you want to check in your e-mail for alerts or to have them pop out at you?

RSS readers come in a variety of forms. Some are free but will display ads or restrict the number of feeds. Others have a fee. A good guide to RSS readers for different platforms can be found at *http://allrss.com/rssreaders.html*.

What you need to be able to set up alerts, and filters, and RSS

The instructions for creating, managing, and deleting alerts and filters are pretty straightforward. Usually you need an account to the service that is offering the alert or filter but these are usually free.

How to find alerts, filters, and RSS

Again, to make the distinction between alerts, filters, and RSS readers:

Alerts: sign up with your e-mail address and, as with an e-mail list, you get messages sent to your e-mail. Generally, everyone who signs up for the alert will get the same material.

Filters: A profile is set up to specify topics of interest. Items which match that profile will be sent to your e-mail.

RSS: An RSS reader program is installed on your computer which you then "populate" with the addresses or RSS links of content you want to be kept updated on.

Here is how a variety of Web sites make their alerts available:

Washington Post: Create a page ("mywashingtonpost") with the sections you are most interested in and when you go to the Washington Post site, you will get your personalized edition. *www.mywashingtonpost.com*

New York Times: Create up to 20 e-mail alerts with "News Tracker," based on your selected topics or keywords. You will get e-mail with links to the articles that fit the profile. You have to be a member of "Times Select" to use this service. *http://select.nytimes.com/mem/tnt.html*

Chicago Tribune: RSS feed. *www.chicagotribune.com/services/site/chi-rsspromo-htmlstory,0,4885820.htmlstory*

BBC: Alerts. Choose from a ticker tape or hourly pop-ups. *http://news.bbc.co.uk/1/hi/help/3533099.stm*

U.S. State Department: Alerts. Receive e-mail updates on travel alerts, speeches and appointments of the Secretary of State, foreign affairs interests and more. *www.state.gov/misc/echannels/66822.htm*

Alerts

Many news Web sites and increasing numbers of government agency sites provide alert services. Finding them is another issue. The links to information on how to sign up for news alerts can be hidden within cluttered homepages. Sometimes the best bet is to check out the "site map" for the Web site and see if there is an alert service link listed.

Bill Dedman's Power Reporting site has a list of alert services, categorized by subject, that would be of interest to journalists at *http://powerreporting.com/category/Alerts_for_journalists*.

Filters

- **Individual.com**: *www.individual.com*. "Individual.com receives thousands of articles from over 70 major news sources each day. We then process and categorize this news into over 200 topics. You get to select 100 of these topics to include in your personalized edition of Individual.com."

- **Google Personalized News**: *http://news.google.com*. Go to "Personalize this Page" to create your own news page, filtered by the topics you select. You will go to this customized news page to see your personal edition.

- **Google Alerts**: *www.google.com/alerts*. Called alerts, but really a customized news filter. Select the words you want Google to find in updates and get a list sent to your e-mail address.

RSS readers

- **Feedreader**: *www.feedreader.com*. Free.

- **Bloglines**: *www.bloglines.com*. Free.

- **NetNewsWire for Mac**: *http://ranchero.com/netnewswire*. Thirty-day free trial for Mac OS, then $29.95.

Exercises

- Figure out a topic you are interested in and set up a news filter at Google Alerts: *www.google.com/alerts*.

- Find out if the Treasury and the Department of Homeland Security have alerts, filters, or RSS feeds.

FOR MORE INFORMATION

Wikipedia entry on RSS
http://en.wikipedia.org/wiki/RSS_%28file_format%29

BLOGS

Blogs (a contraction of "Web logs") are the subject of a great deal of media coverage. But the term is one of those catchall words that really is referring to a number of different things.

Blogs are created using blogging software (there are a variety of programs) that make possible the easy publication of reverse chronological listings of entries. The software also facilitates comments and responses to blog entries by readers, enables categorization and organization of blog entries into topics, and offers other functions that make this a popular self-publishing format.

It is the styles and intentions of blogs that are very different. The format has become exceedingly popular; there are estimates of up to 60 million blogs published (how many of them are maintained or regularly updated is another question).

Following are some of the types of bloggers and uses of the blogs they write:

- **Personal diarists:** Many blogs are used by individuals simply to create a personal diary, a discussion of their days, their likes and dislikes. These tend to be done by younger people. Personal blogs can be useful to journalists particularly if someone who has written a blog ends up in the news, giving the reporter an opportunity for insight into their personality and feelings.

- **Early responders:** Blogging has been a powerful means of getting early reporting out of places and situations where mainstream media coverage is delayed. The early reports and photos of the tsunami in Southeast Asia and the levee breaks in New Orleans came from bloggers. The organization of the blog with latest entry first makes for a great way to post and get the freshest reports. Blogs started in response to a disaster or other situation provide "first person" reports and a unique historical record.

- **Advocates:** People interested in swaying public opinion or who have a political agenda are probably the types of bloggers most people think of when they hear the word. These bloggers have had great political influence and have brought down several high-profile politicians and media personalities when they've waged their campaigns of negative publicity or calling to task for reporting or actions.

- **Hunter/gatherers:** Some bloggers are simply interested in acting as an editorial filter to the Web and use their blogs as a way to let people know about interesting things they have found. There is usually minimal editorializing, just pointing to interesting items culled from the Web. Links are provided to the items. Bloggers with a specific subject interest (environment or a certain band or an industry) are great resources for journalists who are also covering that area.

- **Columnists:** The blog format is increasingly being adopted by news organizations who will have a columnist write a blog for their Web site. Columnists' blogs tend to use more informal language than the equivalent column in the newspaper and some invite public response to the blog entries, creating a conversation that doesn't exist in print.

Uses of blogs in reporting

Particularly in the category of early responders, blogs can provide a unique and critical take on events as they are unfolding. They are also great ways to locate people who have experience with the situation who can be contacted for more in-depth interviewing.

The influence of advocate bloggers as watchdogs of the watchdogs is also interesting. In many cases the advocate bloggers are digging up information and evidence about things happening in the news that really should be reality-checked by journalists.

Checking the blogosphere for entries written by people in the news should be a routine stop for journalists, just as checking for newsgroup messages or personal Web pages should be.

If you are a beat reporter, finding and RSSing a couple of hunter/gatherer bloggers who are tracking the topic you are interested in would be a great way to stay fresh and get some interesting leads.

Blog usage anecdotes

Fargo sex offender, kidnapper, and murderer Joseph Duncan had been writing a blog on Blogspot since January 2004. "Blogging the Fifth Nail" (*http://fifthnail. blogspot.com*) was an account of the mundane details and frustrations of his life, and of the ongoing struggle he had with his demons, maintained until his murderous rampage and kidnappings in May 2005. This is an excellent example of the need to root around in all the corners and alleys of the Web when someone appears in the news. No public records search or other documents could bring as compelling an insight into this man's mind than his blog entries.

How to find blogs

There are a couple of great search engines for blog entries: Technorati (*www.technorati.com*) and Google's Blog Search (*http://blogsearch.google.com*).

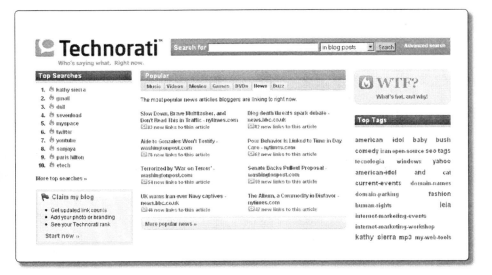

Technorati claims to be indexing 28.9 million blogs. It, too, is almost real-time indexing, taking in the feeds of millions of blogs and getting pointers to new entries into the database continually.

Google's blog search is indexing any blogs that have RSS feeds regardless of what blog service it is on. The blog index dates back to June 2005.

Tips and tricks when using blogs

One of the troubles with scanning blogs is the same as searching for anything on the Web—the volume. Sorting through the chaff to get to some entry of importance is difficult. One thing that can help is to use the "sort by relevance" option in Google, or the "authority" ranking on Technorati, with which you can determine what kinds of hits you will get based on the number of other blogs that linked to that entry (more links, more "authority").

One of the tricks with using a blog is knowing who actually wrote it. Some bloggers provide good background profiles, others are anonymous. Increasingly, public relations companies and spin doctors are using blog space to advocate, so it can be hard to answer the basic questions of "who is this person," "how do they know what they claim to know," and "why are they telling me these things."

What you need to be able to use blogs

Most blogs are RSS ready—if you want to be made aware of new entries to the blog, having an RSS reader set up with that blog listed will give you the updates. There are some blogging services that require you to sign up before you can read the blogs on the service. Otherwise, blogs are simply Web pages formatted using blog software.

Exercises

- Find a blog that is tracking news from Venezuela, particularly about Hugo Chavez.

- Find a blog that gathers news about ecological design or "green" architecture.

FOR MORE INFORMATION

Kline, David and Dan Burnstein. *Blog!: How the Newest Media Revolution is Changing Politics, Business, and Culture.* New York: CDS Books, 2005.

Scott, D. Travers. "Blog Invasion! What are They? Where Did They Come From?" May 26, 2004. *http://homepage.mac.com/dtraversscott/Academics/BlogHistory/BlogsScott.pdf*

Bialik, Carl. "Measuring the Impact of Blogs Requires More than Counting." WSJ Online, May 26, 2005. *http://online.wsj.com/public/article/ SB111685593903640572-DoCm_P_b1HHSoXRla2QEob6bw8w_20060525.html*

WIKIS

Wikis (derived from the Hawaiian term "wikiwiki," which means quick) are created using a particular software program (there are several Wiki programs) which allows instant updating of content pages. These are collaborative publishing spaces which make it possible for anyone to go in and edit and immediately see the changed pages. The edits of the pages are tracked so anyone can see where content was changed and who changed it.

Wikis are controversial spaces in that there are questions about authorship and credibility. However, the largest of the Wiki publications, the Wikipedia, has become a valuable and unique information space. The Wikipedia, "the free encyclopedia that anyone can edit," has over 1 million entries in the English version alone. Count the articles written in all 100 languages in Wikipedia and there are over 3,800,000 articles. There are 13,000 active "Wikipedians."

Not only is Wikipedia collaboratively written but it is collaboratively edited. People intensely interested in a particular topic will "babysit" the content and monitor when changes happen to the page to make sure the content isn't maliciously changed. The real beauty of the Wikipedia project is that it is an opportunity for collective intelligence to record information about all sorts of topics large and small. People have taken on creating encyclopedic content on everything from the Ottoman Empire to Wacker Avenue in Chicago.

There is an additional Wiki project called Wikinews that has not taken off as strongly as Wikipedia. The idea was that this would be a place where "citizen reporters" could post news about what is happening in their town or community.

There is editorial control as this message about a recent "Story in Development" indicates:

> "This article has been nominated for **editorial cleanup**, that is, an editor considers it not to be publishable in its current form. The following reason has been cited 'Article may be a hoax, please provide a specific example of this ever occurring from a reputable source. Otherwise, this whole issue may have never happened.'"

Wiki software is also being used to do collaborative thinking and project planning in newsrooms, companies, and schools. The content space allows easy version control since everyone sees the same thing, everyone can see what gets edited or added, and everyone can see who made the changes.

Uses of Wikis in reporting

Increasingly, and much to the chagrin of scholars and information elitists, if you put a term into Google the Wikipedia entry might be the first hit to come up. For complex topics, the reliability of this information may or may not be on par with a more traditionally edited reference. But for obscure topics and places, this might be a very valuable reference.

The Online Journalism Review is making clever use of Wiki software with its online tutorials on journalism skills: *www.ojr.org/ojr/wiki*. These articles (on ethics, writing for the Web, reporting a news story online, etc.) are being collaboratively written and edited.

How to find Wikis

- **WikiIndex**: *www.wikiindex.com*. WikiIndex is a growing directory of operating Wikis organized by topic, language, status (active or not), and Wiki engine used.

- **"How Wikis Work"**: *http://computer.howstuffworks.com/wiki.htm*. This article from "How Stuff Works" explains how Wiki communities work and the problems of collaborative content-building.

Tips and tricks when using Wikis

Consider the source(s). For topics that are charged with agenda or political bias, Wikipedia entries can be an interesting source of perspective, but not necessarily of facts or unbiased interpretation. For other topics, checking to see when the information was entered and updated will help you ensure you have recent information. If you are looking at a Wiki entry about Roman coins, the information probably isn't that time sensitive or particularly bias-ridden, but an entry about Rome's current political situation might be well be both.

What you need to be able to use Wikis

- If you just want to read Wikipedia or Wikinews, you can just go to the site. If you want to update an entry, you may need to subscribe or register.

- If you want to create your own Wiki for a collaborative project, you can go to a Wiki service like TWiki (*www.twiki.org*), set up an account, and build your own. Usually a simple Wiki with only a few authorized users is free. To make unlimited access or a large amount pages available, there is a fee.

Exercises

- Think of a topic about which you are particularly knowledgeable. Check out the entry on that topic in Wikipedia (*www.wikipedia.org*) and in Encarta (*http://encarta.msn.com*). What differences do you see?

- You're looking for a good graphic about the eruption of Mount Vesuvius in Pompeii. Look in the Wikipedia entry on Pompeii and see if you can use any of the graphics on the page.

FOR MORE INFORMATION

Sreenivasan, Sree. "Wikipedia for Journalists: Trusting a Free Resource."
Poynter Online. Mar. 8, 2004.
www.poynter.org/column.asp?id=32&aid=62126

Glasner, Joanna. "Wikipedia Creators Move Into News." Wired News. Nov. 29,
2004. *www.wired.com/news/culture/0,1284,65819,00.html*

Mayfield, Kendra. "Not Your Father's Encyclopedia." Wired News. Jan. 28,
2003. *www.wired.com/news/culture/0,1284,57364,00.html*

SOCIAL NETWORK SERVICES

A good definition of social network services comes from Wikipedia:

> "A social network service is social software specifically focused on the building and verifying of social networks for whatever purpose. As of 2005, there are over three hundred known social networking Web sites. Some help people to come together online around shared interests or causes. For example, some dating services let users post their personal profiles, location, age, gender, etc, and help them search for a partner. Similarly, some social bookmarking services allow users to post their list of bookmarks—or favorite Web sites—for others to search and view, so that they can locate resources identified as useful by others who share the same interests."

In addition, Social Network Analysis is a computer-assisted reporting technique, which involves identifying connections between people through input of information into social network analysis software. This is a powerful new reporting tool to show connections in corporate relationships, terror networks, and other situations by understanding who knows whom and through what link. IRE offers great information about this use of social networking at *www.ire.org/sna*.

Uses of social network services in reporting

Most social networking services can be searched by a variety of categories of interest or detail about the person. If you are looking for sources within a particular age range, location, or who have specific interests, you could search in a social network service and find some good people to contact.

Finding people who knew the people who find themselves in the news is easily done by searching connections on a social networking site. Examples of social networking sites are Facebook, MySpace, and Tribe. Most of these are extremely popular with young people. Adults are more likely to be found on the sites that cater to specific interests or in business networking services like LinkedIn.

Social networking anecdotes

We tapped into our social network of reporters through the IRE listserv and got these great anecdotes about how social networking services have been useful in reporting.

Erin Einhorn, a reporter at New York Daily News, told about how a colleague used a social networking site entry in their reporting of corruption in City Hall for the Philadelphia Daily News:

> "When federal investigators were crawling around Philadelphia's City Hall as part of a corruption investigation and they were zeroing in on a city treasurer who had mysteriously and suddenly quit, someone whispered to one of my colleagues that he had a page on blackplanet. com. His picture on the site confirmed it was him. It didn't advance the corruption story, but we learned a) that the guy was fishing for women with a wife and three kids at home and b) that he was inflating his resume on the site (claiming he was the finance director of a major U.S. city, as opposed to merely treasurer). It seemed off-topic (and, frankly, a mean intrusion into the guy's personal life) but two years later during his trial (he was convicted), one of the witnesses against him was a woman he met on that site."

Matt Wynn, IRE Data Analyst, sent these anecdotes about social networking services uses by reporters at the Missourian:

- When a football player died on the field, [reporters] checked his "wall" on Facebook to find RIP messages and people who were close to him. Not only did they confirm the death, they reached valuable sources, too.

- When a freshman committed suicide by jumping from an eighth-story window, [reporters] used Facebook to reach people who knew him.

- In one of the stranger incidents, a group of fraternity brothers took part in some vandalism of some sort, then bragged about the arrest and the crime on their Facebook accounts. Their comments put the crime into perspective and, in fact, turned into a story on their own.

- The profile of a student who was running for vice-president of the student body included a photo of her duct-taped to a chair with a beer bong down her throat. After a newspaper broke that story, she pulled out of the race.

Ryan Blitstein, a staff writer at SF Weekly, shared some great insights about social networking in a column by Sree Sreenivasan in Poynter Online (*www.poynter.org/column.asp?id=32&aid=91496*). They agreed we could share them here:

> Friendster, MySpace, and Tribe are a 21st-century version of a little black book, calendar, photo album, diary, and telephone rolled into one. Everybody's information is public and, better yet, searchable, if you know where to look. Recently, I needed to find sources that fit a specific profile: Asian Americans who graduated from a certain San Francisco high school during the last few years. I focused on MySpace, the music-centered site that has become the online equivalent of the suburban mall for teenagers and college students. I registered, creating a simple MySpace profile (Ryan, Journalist, San Francisco). Then, under the Search option, I chose users who went to the school, narrowing the list to recent graduates. Several dozen profiles remained, many of which listed "Asian" under ethnicity. Sites also let you search by occupation, location, even last name.

> Social network reporting isn't without drawbacks, logistically and ethically. Many site users, despite what their profiles say, are under 18, so use the same caution you would when reporting on high school kids. Be aware that most people don't expect their profiles to be read by anyone other than their friends, much less to be cold-e-mailed by a journalist. Some of those I contacted responded as if someone had stolen and read their private diary. It's also a good idea, if you already have a profile, to create a new one for reporting—after all, you don't want sources discovering any of your private information.

How to find social network services

The Social Software Weblog maintains a categorized list of social networking services at *http://socialsoftware.Weblogsinc.com/2005/02/14/home-of-the-social-networking-services-meta-list*. There are business networking sites and "common interest" networking sites.

Tips and tricks when using social network services

Note the caution Ryan Blitstein stated above about using information from these sites—particularly if the people are underage (or say they are).

Understand that all of the information is contributed by the person in the profile, none of it is "fact-checked," much of it will be presented to enhance the person's image (or so they think). This can be a great locator tool but it will require actual communication with the source to get any real useful information.

What you need to be able to use social network services

Most social network services are free for the basic service but you will have to register. In some cases, you have to set up a profile of yourself before you can search for others. Some services require that you are a member of a certain community (for example, to use Facebook you used to have to have an e-mail address ending with .edu.)

Exercise

- Sign up for Friendster or MySpace and find people from your town.

FOR MORE INFORMATION

Duffy, Jonathan. "The MySpace Age." BBC Online. March 7, 2006.
http://news.bbc.co.uk/2/hi/uk_news/magazine/4782118.stm

Sreenivasan, Sree. "Social Networking for Journalists." Poynter Online. Nov. 9,
2005. *www.poynter.org/column.asp?id=32&aid=91496*

Now that we've discussed the various and sundry tools the Internet makes available, in the next chapter we will discuss in more depth the resources found on the World Wide Web. We will also delve into the search techniques that will help you locate resources on the Web or in these kinds of resources that were detailed here in Chapter 2.

Chapter 3

World Wide Web

The World Wide Web is the epicenter of content on the Internet. Chapter 2 introduced many of the tools that allow you to use the Internet for communication, surveillance of the news environment, and networking. This chapter will introduce many of the features of the content sites on the World Wide Web.

WWW contents

Think of the World Wide Web as a big circle. Slice the circle into three parts. These three slices represent the contents of the World Wide Web.

One part contains Web sites with valuable, useful, and credible information.

One part contains Web sites that help you locate those Web sites with information.

The final part is trash, porn, propaganda, and personal pages about people's pets. (Unfortunately, this might be the biggest slice of the three.)

As a journalist or researcher using the Web, you'll want to concentrate on the first two parts and figure out how to recognize and avoid the last part. This section will describe the valuable information content Web sites, where they come from, and how to use them. The next section will go into the different kinds of Web sites that help you find these content sites. In the section on Web searching basics you will get advice on how to search efficiently for materials from the useful part of the Web and avoid the stuff that wastes your time.

How to recognize Web content sites

The most important clue in recognizing Web sites with useful content and information is to look at the "top level domain" (TLD) indicated in the suffix of the Web address. The TLD is usually the last part of the Web address, such as .com, .gov, or .edu. The TLD will give you clues about the source of the Web site. Knowing these TLDs and how to use them in searching for Web sites (see the section of this chapter on searching) will help make your Web use more efficient.

There are currently 17 TLDs that indicate different kinds of domains used for Web sites. The UK and some other countries use slight variations of these domains. Different countries also use country codes as suffixes to indicate country of origin. You can find the list of country domains at *www.iana.org/cctld/cctld-whois.htm*.

The current domain types are:

- **.aero**: air-transport industry sites

- **.biz**: restricted to businesses (added after .com became too undifferentiated)

- **.cat**: for Catalan linguistic and cultural community sites

- **.com**: commercial sites

- **.coop**: cooperative association sites

- **.edu**: primarily accredited postsecondary education sites, although some K-12 sites may have .edu in the domain as well

- **.gov**: U.S. government sites; some other countries use .gov followed by their country code (e.g. .au for Australia, .cn for China)

- **.info**: sites with information about companies, products, or ideas

- **.int**: organizations established by international treaties

- **.jobs**: human resource managers' sites

- **.mil**: reserved exclusively for U.S. military sites

- **.mobi**: sites for consumers and providers of mobile products and services

- **.museum**: sites for museums

- **.name**: sites for individuals

- **.net**: sites for networks

- **.org**: sites for primarily noncommercial communities and associations

- **.pro**: sites for credentialed professionals and related entities

- **.travel**: sites for entities whose primary area of activity is in the travel industry

There has been such growth on the Web that the current name registration system is always under discussion. The Internet Corporation for Assigned Names and Numbers (ICANN) is responsible for managing the name registration protocols, and changes are usually subject to wide discussion and debate in the Internet community before being adopted.

Other Web address conventions helpful in identifying Web sites:

State government sites: *www.state.**.us*
** stands for the two-letter state code, like the one used by the Postal Service. For example, the State of New York's web site is *www.state.ny.us*. Find state abbreviations on the U.S. Postal Service site at *www.usps.gov/ncsc*.

State-level government agencies: *www.***.state.**.us*
*** stands for the agency acronym, and the ** is the state abbreviation. For example, the Minnesota State Legislature's Web site is *www.leg.mn.us*.

County government sites: *www.co.******.**.us*
****** stands for the county name or abbreviated name, and the ** is the state abbreviation. For example, the Pima County, Arizona, Web site is *www.co.pima.az.us*.

City government sites: *www.ci.*****.**.us*
***** is the city name, and ** is the state abbreviation. For example, the City of Seattle's Web site is *www.ci.seattle.wa.us*.

FOR MORE INFORMATION

Top-Level Domains
www.icann.org/tlds

WHO PUBLISHES WEB SITES WITH CONTENT

The domain names identify the categories of Web sites with content, but these need to be broken down a bit more. The following pages outline the types of sponsors of Web sites with content of value to journalists and researchers. We'll look at each type, what kind of information they provide and why, the use journalists can make of those sites, tips and traps in using the sites, and some ways to locate those types of sites. You will notice that these sites correspond to the four types of sources described in Chapter 1: informal, institutional, scholarly and journalistic.

- **Individuals** (informal sources)

- **Government agencies** (institutional sources)

- **Organizations and associations** (institutional sources)

- **Commercial enterprises/businesses** (institutional sources)

- **Military** (institutional sources)

- **Educational institutions** (scholarly sources)

- **News organizations/publications** (journalistic sources)

- **Libraries** (contain materials from all fours types of sources)

INDIVIDUALS

Anyone can register for a Web domain, and they do. The number of Web sites that let people create their own Web pages is growing and so, too, are the number of individuals taking advantage of these services. Today anyone can be a publisher. Individuals' Web sites are the informal sources that provide the color, the "ring true" factor, the personality to your stories. Individuals' hobbies, philosophies, obsessions, and experiences are all out there on the Web. Much of the third slice of the Web—the trash, porn, mis-information, and just plain drivel—comes from individuals. But there are also some very useful resources compiled by individuals. It takes some looking and a lot of evaluation once you find them, but these informal sources can be a goldmine.

You can often recognize a personal/individual's pages by the tilde (or ~) in the address (e.g. *http://home.att.net/~johndoe*). On GeoCities alone (*http://geocities.yahoo.com*) millions of people have created personal pages. There are hundreds of Web locations offering space for people who want to create their own sites.

Add to these the blogs written and maintained by individuals and you have even more potential contributions from informal sources. Blog hosting sites like Blogspot, EasyJournal, and LiveJournal make the creation of individual blogs easy and abundant.

Types of information they provide

The range of interests and topics that individuals write about covers everything under the sun: Information about stars, singers, athletes. Compilations of links on strange and interesting topics. Stories about personal experiences. Products someone wants to sell. Background on hobbies or collections. Personal biographies (complete with pictures of the family and pets) and family genealogies.

Why they provide it

The Web has become the ultimate vanity press. This is a way for people to "share" their life's interest, their obsessions. What in the past might have been a newsletter sent to a few people is now a Web site available to the world. Some are inspired by philanthropic instinct, and they feel the information they have is important to share. Some really do just seem to have too much time on their hands. This is the "good news and bad news" of the Web—anyone can publish anything and *anyone* can publish *anything*.

Uses in reporting and research

- Looking for something off-beat? Want to find the fringe? Individual pages can help.

- Personal pages are becoming so common that checking to see if someone you are covering has created a page should be part of your backgrounding routine. (Young people involved in news events of various kinds—good or bad—may have personal pages that provide an insight into their worldview.)

- Looking for people with personal experience? Personal Web pages and blogs are a great way to locate people who want to share their experiences.

Tips and traps

- Figuring out who put the page together, what their qualifications are, and why they've done it (key criteria for evaluating Web sites) is often very difficult to do. You may need to send an e-mail message to the creator of the site to ask some qualifying questions.

- It may look authoritative but it is not necessarily. No one has checked the material on these pages. Browser beware.

- Compilations and information on individuals' pages may have been a one-time interest but are no longer being kept up to date. Always check when the page was last modified to see how fresh it is.

- Many universities give space on the computer server to students, and they usually don't monitor the contents. Generally, information on .edu sites (educational sites) can be considered reliable unless the URL has a ~ in the address, which indicates this is a personal page sitting on the educational site server.

- Be careful when using "personal pages" (or reading profiles) purported to be of someone who is suddenly the focus of media attention. Hoax postings or profiles by people in the spotlight are not uncommon.

Exercises for personal pages

- You're doing a feature story on strange collections and hobbies. Find collectors of telephones, subway tokens, and antique postcards. Use the Webring Directory: *www.webring.org*.

- You're a photographer and are assigned to shoot a "pick your favorite band" concert. Go to some fan sites and find out something about the performances they give. Check out some photos.

- Find some personal pages relating to scoliosis. Why might you use these in reporting? Why wouldn't you use them?

Finding personal pages

- The directories on sites which provide personal page services are good places to look. The search functions on GeoCities (*http://geocities.yahoo.com/search*) and Tripod (*www.tripod.lycos.com*) taps into the interests of hundreds of thousands of people.

- Technorati (*www.technorati.com*) and Google's Blogsearch (*http://blogsearch. google.com*) are two great sources for finding blogs.

- The Web search engines (Google, AltaVista, Yahoo, etc.) index personal home pages. A large portion of the items retrieved from a search come from individuals. There are also directories of all kinds of specific types of personal pages (by profession, geographic region, religion). If you are looking for a particular type of person's pages, search for "home page" and the keyword you are looking for.

- Personal Pages Worldwide: College and University Collections: *www.utexas. edu/world/personal*
  Links to college directories of student home pages on the college's server.

- Yahoo! Personal Home Pages: *http://dir.yahoo.com/Society_and_Culture/ People/Personal_Home_Pages*
  More than 17,000 personal pages by name.

- Web rings are made up primarily of personal pages. Find Web rings (see more on Web rings in the next chapter) at *www.webring.org*.

GOVERNMENT AGENCIES

Government agencies were some of the earliest users of the Web and now most government agencies and branches, from local city government up to national governmental departments around the world, have some level of representation on the Web. These are among the most prolific and important institutional sources for journalists.

United States federal government Web sites can be identified by the .gov at the end of the Web address. (See page 91 for the Web address structure for state and local government agencies.)

Types of information they provide

Reports, statistics, texts of speeches, documents, data, personnel directories and biographical information, forms, and information about the structure and activities of the agency.

Why they provide it

Part of the responsibility of the federal government is information distribution. In some cases, information release is mandated by federal law. Federal agencies and offices need to inform citizens about their activities and provide ways to get involved. Government Web sites are an economical way to provide access to the information these important institutions have compiled.

Uses in reporting and research

- Go to interviews with background and facts that your source may not want to tell you.

- Provide a reality check for information gleaned from interviews or other reports. Read the text of speeches and find voting records when covering legislators to see if their statements and votes match.

- Find experts in agencies through directories.

- Find statistics that help illustrate a point you are trying to make or put an event into a broader context.

- Get alerts and news releases from agencies.

- Get information from the agency after agency hours or when no one is available.

Tips and traps

- Information found on government sites is as reliable and credible as it would be distributed through any other medium. If you would use the agency as a source, you can trust the information found on its Web site.

- Information on government Web sites usually does not pre-date the Web— about 1995. If you want older information you'll need to contact the agency or go to a regional government document repository library.

- Government agencies often distribute the latest information and reports via their Web site, but not always. Locating a report on the Web should be followed up with a call to the agency to see if there is new information not yet released. The Web does not automatically make data more current if the agency hasn't released new information. Don't get frustrated that the most current report on a topic cites 2004 data—government moves slowly.

- There is no consistent way of organizing information used on government sites. You will have to look over the sections and features carefully to get a sense of the types and arrangements of information. Check the "site map" of an agency site to get an easily-browsed table of contents.

- Your first stop when learning the Web should be to your local and state government sites so you can learn what information is readily available to you.

Exercises for government sites

- You are a business reporter and hear that the largest employer in your town is going to be laying off one-third of its employees. You need to background the company's financial status. Find the latest 10-K filings for a large public company in your area. Use the EDGAR (Electronic Data Gathering, Analysis, and Retrieval) database from the Securities and Exchange Commission: *www. sec.gov/edgar.shtml.*

- In a story on an "English-only" referendum being proposed, you want to add information about the demographics of your county, particularly the Hispanic population. Search for population statistics for your county on the Census Bureau Web site: *www.census.gov.*

- You're doing a story on Medicare reform and want to include quotes by the president on the topic. Look for mentions of "Medicare" in the president's speeches and addresses at the White House site: *www.whitehouse.gov.*

- You are the education writer and the new Superintendent of Schools is from Bahrain. You want to do some research on his educational background in Bahrain. Find out about the education system in Bahrain from its Ministry of Education: *www.education.gov.bh.*

- In covering a story about domestic violence in Florida, a cop tells you that the hot weather months are the worst—there is a jump in cases in July. Verify the accuracy of his statement by checking the Florida Department of Children and Families Web site: *www.state.fl.us/cf_web.*

EDGAR Company Search

From this page, you can search the EDGAR database for company information, including real-time filings. If more than one company name matches your search keyword(s), you will be presented with a list of possible matches from which to pick. Company filings are available for **1993** through **2006**. See also our EDGAR Full-Text Search.

Enter your search information:

Company name: `Target`

or CIK or Ticker Symbol: *(Central Index Key)*
(Tickers for 9600 largest publicly traded companies)

or File Number:

or State: *(two-letter abbreviation)*

and/or SIC:

and Ownership Forms 3, 4, and 5? ⦿ Include ◯ Exclude ◯ Only

[Find Companies]

FOR MORE INFORMATION

Garvin, Peggy, ed. *Government Information on the Internet*. 6th ed. Lanham, MD: Bernan Associates, 2003.

Johnson, Dennis. *Congress Online: Bridging the Gap Between Citizens and their Representatives*. Oxford, UK: Routledge, 2004.

Martin, Mary, ed. *Local and Regional Government Information: How to Find It, How to Use It*. Westport, CT: Greenwood Press, 2005.

Finding government sites

- **A – Z Index of U.S. Government Departments and Agencies**: *www.usa.gov/Agencies/Federal/All_Agencies/index.shtml*

- **State and Local Government on the Net**: *www.statelocalgov.net*

- **Foreign Government Resources on the Web**: *www.lib.umich.edu/govdocs/foreign.html* (Last updated in July 2006.)

- **Political Science Resources on the Web**: *www.lib.umich.edu/govdocs/polisci.html*

- **Guess**. Use your knowledge of Web addressing for government sites to guess what the address might be for a particular agency. Where, for example, would you find the Internal Revenue Service?

ORGANIZATIONS AND ASSOCIATIONS

Every issue, philosophy, physical disease, occupation, and recreational activity is represented by some group or another. You can recognize organization sites from the .org at the end of the address. These institutions are typically involved in advocating a cause or promoting a point of view. Many of them are non-profit institutions, but you cannot assume that is so just because the organization's Web address uses the .org domain. The typical rule of thumb applies: don't assume, check it out.

Types of information they provide

Brochures and pamphlets, fund-raising information, activities they are involved in, information about directors and others involved in the organization, professional publications and newsletters, research reports, and statistics.

Why they provide it

Associations want to provide information about their organization and their activities. They want to promote their cause and spread information about their particular position on topics.

Uses in reporting and research

- Find experts and researchers.

- Find background information and statistics on topics.

- Uncover various facets of an issue by checking a number of different associations' positions.

- Get story ideas by checking news releases from associations.

Tips and traps

- Associations have a position they are promoting; make sure you understand their agenda when evaluating the information they provide on the site.

- There are a number of different associations on the same issue or topic. Be sure to look at the positions represented by a number of them to get all the angles on the topic.

- For many organizations, the Web site is a sideline, not their main activity, so updating material may be a secondary concern. Use the Web site to get a sense of activities and positions but call them to find out their latest information.

- The domain .org used to be more controlled, only real non-profits could get that domain. But that is no longer the case. Anyone can apply for the .org domain. Be careful when checking the credentials of a Web site with .org.

Exercises for association sites

- Oh, the irony. One of Greenpeace's ships, the Esperanza, collided with a fishing vessel and spilled thousands of gallons of fuel into the North Sea. Find information about the ship on the Web site (and figure out for yourself what the Web address would be).

- You do the medical briefs column and want to focus on new developments in cancer treatment. Go to the American Cancer Society Web site and find some news releases: *www.cancer.org*.

- You are doing a story about Morris Dees, one of the co-founders of the Southern Poverty Law Center. You need a bio. Find one at the SPLC site: *www.splcenter.org*.

- A candidate for state treasurer said she is a proponent of bionomics. What in the world is bionomics and who could you interview about it?

Finding association sites

- The Internet Public Libraries listing of Associations on the Net (*www.ipl.org/ div/AON*) groups associations by topics and has a great search engine to locate relevant associations.

- If you are looking for a specific organization, the best way to find it might be to just guess the address. Knowing the suffix is .org and the prefix is usually www, try to guess which word or acronym might be the middle part.

- If you are looking for any association that might deal with the subject you are interested in, try guessing the address. Put *www.***.org* with the *** being the topic you are looking for. Give it a try.

- Use a search engine and search for "association" and "topic" (the subject you are looking for) and see what sorts of esoteric associations turn up. Or use a field search (see the section on searching) and look for sites with .org in the address along with the topic you are interested in.

Checking out charities

- **GuideStar**: *www.guidestar.org*
  Information on more than 650,000 nonprofit organizations

- **Better Business Bureau Wise Giving Alliance**: *www.give.org*
  Information about charity expenditures, for use by donors who want to know
  how their dollars are spent.

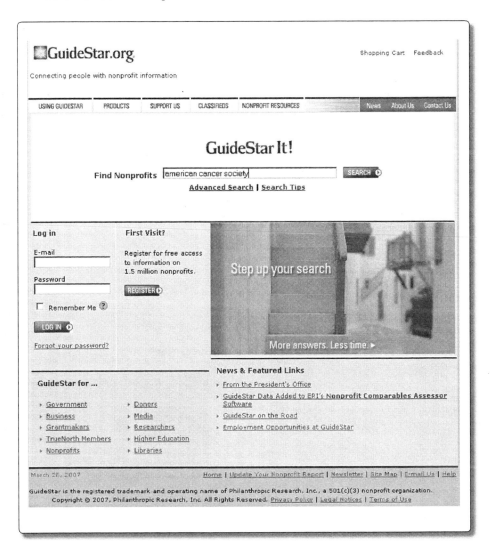

COMMERCIAL ENTERPRISES/BUSINESSES

Most business enterprises, from mom and pops to major corporations, have a virtual storefront on the Web.

The .com domain has become so large that the .biz and .info domains were added in the early 2000s to provide some differentiation and expand the address options.

Commercial sites are identified by the .com at the end. The .biz domain is for businesses. The .info domain is for information about companies, products, or ideas. For British and some other non-U.S. sites, the address will use ".co" then the two-letter country code.

Types of information they provide

Product information, biographical and contact information on officers of the company, financial information, annual reports, and suggestions on how to use the products they sell. Many commercial sites provide online shopping services as well as information about their physical locations. Most major companies maintain "press rooms" online with news releases and other updated company information.

Why they provide it

They are promoting their products, providing opportunities for purchasing products, and making information about their company available to investors and possible employees. The sites also support their public relations needs by making press releases available. Federal and state governments require publicly-held companies to file some information with them to safeguard shareholders and oversee regulatory requirements.

Uses in reporting and research

- Background information about companies.

- Biographical information about corporate officers.

- When there is a breaking story, getting information from the site might be faster than going through the public relations officer.

- Get information after hours or on weekends when there's no one to answer questions.

- Annual reports or financial information for publicly-held companies.

Tips and traps

- The range of information on business sites can vary. Sometimes they provide very up-to-date information, and sometimes the data are old. Always check for more recent information by calling the company.

- These are promotional sites, they want to put the best spin on their company and their activities—remember that when looking at the information. No one is monitoring their site for credibility or for false claims.

- Annual reports on corporate sites are frequently in Adobe Acrobat format (PDF). You'll need to download the Acrobat reader to be able to view those documents.

Exercises for business sites

- The mid-section emergency exit door of a U.S. Airways Airbus A320 blows out. What rows of the airplane were nearest the door? Look for the seating charts on the U.S. Airways site: *www.usairways.com.*

- Wal-Mart is planning on building a supercenter in your town and there is considerable public opposition. Can you find anything at the company's Web site about how they have handled these controversies in other cities?

- You're a health and nutrition columnist and are doing a column on the fat content of fast foods. Check out the nutrition information on the Burger King, McDonald's, and Wendy's sites. (Find the Web addresses, and remember, there are no punctuation marks in addresses.)

Finding business sites

- **BizWeb**: *www.bizweb.com*
  Links to more than 46,000 businesses listed by category.

- **Annual Reports Gallery**: *www.reportgallery.com*
  Links to the pages within corporate sites which contain the annual report.

- **Google Finance**: *http://finance.google.com*
  The very comprehensive information on publicly traded companies found in the profiles includes Web site address.

- Many times you can correctly guess the Web address by combining the company name with the .com or .biz domain name.

FOR MORE INFORMATION

Berkman, Robert. *The Skeptical Business Searcher: The Information Advisor's Guide to Evaluating Web Data, Sites, and Sources.* Bedford, NJ: Information Today, 2004.

MILITARY

Considering the amount of money the U.S. federal government allocates to the military and all of its subsidiary activities, it should not come as a surprise that there are many thousands of Web sites that sport the .mil domain name. Military institutions are prolific in their information generation, despite the public's perception that defense-related information is difficult to find and hard to pry loose from government hands.

Types of information they provide

Statistics and specification on equipment and personnel. Background on military bases. History of military units. Veterans' affairs information.

Why they provide it

These are promotional sites and are also used to provide information and support to active personnel and veterans.

Uses in reporting and research

- Get background on different military units.

- Find statistics and background on weapons.

- Find contacts at different bases to interview.

Tips and traps

- Be sure you are looking at an official site. There are lots of military enthusiasts and veterans who create official-looking Web pages but which aren't officially sanctioned. A good clue is official sites will have .mil in the address.

- Don't expect military secrets or internal information to appear on the Web site. These are distribution mechanisms for what the military wants you to know.

Exercises for military sites

- Someone calls and says he works for the Army's Chemical Materials Agency and has some inside information about dangerous procedures at the site in South Dakota. Should you drop everything and talk to him?

- There is an explosion at the U.S. Coast Guard Base in Cape Cod, Massachusetts. Use these two sources to find information about the base: *www.uscg.mil/top/units* and *www.globalsecurity.org/military/facility*. Which one was easier to use? Which had the more reliable information?

- A Harrier GR7 from the UK Royal Air Force crashed into the crowd during an air show demonstration. You need background on the plane. Get a profile from the RAF Web site: *www.raf.mod.uk.*

Finding Military Sites

- **DefenseLINK portal to the U.S. Department of Defense on the Web**: *www.defenselink.mil/sites*

- **SearchMil.com**: *www.searchmil.com*
  More than 1 million military pages indexed and ranked in order of popularity.

- **Federation of American Scientists**: *www.fas.org*
  A military-related portal produced by a respected non-profit organization.

- **MERLN** (the Military Education Research Library Network): *http://merln.ndu.edu*
  A consortium of military education research libraries. The site includes the full text of U.S. military policy documents, legislation, links to worldwide military libraries, and links to military journals and publications.

EDUCATIONAL/SCHOLARLY INSTITUTIONS

The Internet was originally the domain of education. You had to be affiliated with a university or college or think tank to tap into the network of networks. Now, educational and scholarly institutions—from kindergartens to graduate schools—are using the Web not just to communicate with each other, but to promote themselves and share information.

Educational sites can be identified by the .edu in the address. Some non-U.S. educational sites use .ac instead of .edu. Some kindergarten through high schools use the name of the school, location, and ".k12" in the URL, so don't assume the .edu domain will work for every school.

Types of information they provide

Information about departments and courses available, faculty biographies and contact information, directories of faculty expertise, and student directories. Information about admissions and administration. Faculty and student publications and projects. Course syllabi. Some have "virtual tours" of the facilities. Access to information about the school's library collection. Much of the work that is generated by scholarly activity can be found through the Web sites with which the scholars are affiliated.

Why they provide it

They want to attract students and provide promotional information. They want to share studies and research done by faculty. They want to maintain contacts with alumni and raise money.

Uses in reporting and research

- Locate experts through faculty expert directories or course descriptions.

- Get information about the school when covering events that might have happened there.

- Find research reports.

Tips and traps

- These are essentially promotional sites; you won't find too much negative about the college or school there.

- Some school sites contain no more than a brochure about the school would, while others have rich and vast resources available. None of them contain all the material generated by the school, so use these as starting points, not definitive collections.

- Some elementary, middle, and high school sites were taken on as student projects and have not been maintained. Be sure to check the date of the last updates to the page.

Exercises for education sites

- A source tells you that someone named Brownsberger at the Harvard Division on Addictions is a great source to talk to about drug law enforcement. Find him.

- You've been asked by the local university to teach a class on technical writing. Look at some syllabi done by others teaching similar courses at the World Lecture Hall: *http://web.austin.utexas.edu/wlh*.

- You're the education reporter in St. Petersburg, Florida. It's the weekend and you hear a rumor that students at Northeast High are going to stage a huge protest on Monday because of new, restrictive dress codes. You need to talk to someone in the administration. What do you do?

Finding education sites

- **All About College**: *http://allaboutcollege.com*
  Links to colleges and universities by state and country.

- **U.S. Journal of Academics**: *www.usjournal.com*
  Primarily a guide for international students looking for a university, four-year liberal arts college, or community college in the U.S., but a very good guide by location.

- **American School Directory**: *www.asd.com*
  A subscription-based service with information on more than 105,000 K-12 schools in the United States.

NEWS ORGANIZATIONS/PUBLICATIONS

Virtually every large paper and most small ones around the world have created news Web sites. Worldwide there are now more than 5,000 newspaper Web sites. Television and radio stations have Web sites, too. Print-based magazines and a wide range of electronic-only publications (called zines) are also well represented on the Web.

Most of these are .com sites because they are all in the business of information distribution. These sources correspond to the "journalistic sources" described in Chapter 2.

Types of information they provide

Newspaper and the large television and public radio sites provide fairly comprehensive coverage of daily news events. Some offer archives of past stories. They frequently have compilations of local events and entertainment options. Special packages and projects are a feature of some of the large sites. The large television and public radio sites include streaming audio and/or video segments, and some newspaper sites are starting to include more multimedia elements to their stories.

Many of the smaller and regional television and radio sites are mostly promotional, giving information about the anchors and giving the program schedule. They usually also offer news content such as links to video from the news casts.

Magazine sites are usually promotional. They may offer a few of the current issue's articles and some are starting to provide cover-to-cover representation, typically for the previous issue than for the latest one on the newsstand.

Why they provide it

They are in business and their product is information. This is seen as an important outlet for distribution of their product. This is also an important promotional tool about their publications. Many news organizations see Web access to their products as a new revenue stream. They are offering access to previously published stories through Web-accessible archives and news aggregators.

Uses in reporting and research

- **Regional research**: hopping around to different news sites can quickly give you a sense of how stories are playing or what angles are being covered on a story you are doing.

- **Get background on people and events**: Web-accessible news archives can be an inexpensive way of checking background on topics and people.

- **Find out about what's going on in a city you may be visiting**: if you are covering a news event in another town, checking the local media can give you a sense of what is going on there.

- **Get story ideas**: do a quick check of specialty publication Web sites and see what sorts of stories they are doing; you might get some new ideas.

- **Find reporting expertise**: check around on news sites and see who covers the kind of story you are doing. If they aren't in a competing market they may be willing to help with sources and angles.

- **Audio and video**: being able to hear the press conference or see video from the scene can give you additional information you need as you cover a story.

Tips and traps

- If you want information about the parent company of the newspaper, station, or publication you may need to go to a corporate site. Generally there are separate Web sites for the individual publications and stations and another site which has corporate information.

- Here today and gone tomorrow is the modus operandi for far too many news sites. The constantly changing content and, for the most part, inadequate archiving of Web content makes locating past news stories a catch-as-catch-can proposition.

- Searching news archives on Web sites is usually free, that's the good news. The bad news is that if you find an article you want to read, there is usually a charge. You can find articles about the topic you want, that's the good news. But the bad news is the search you did often does not give you very much information about the articles you've retrieved; you sometimes have to look through a number of "hits" before you find what you need.

- Increasingly, news Web sites require registration to get deeper into the site. This is usually free, but it can be a hassle.

Exercises for news and publication sites

- You're doing a story about a local grade school that has launched its own radio station with a low-power FM frequency license. Find out how many other grade schools in the U.S. run radio stations. Use *www.radio-locator.com*.

- Find a local radio, TV, and newspaper site for a town you've lived in before.

- The Minnesota Vikings are leaving Minneapolis and coming to your town. You want to talk to folks who have been covering the Vikings. Find some football/sports writers in Minneapolis or St. Paul.

- You're heading to London for the summer and want to do some writing while you are there. What are some of the big stories going on there right now?

Finding news and publication sites

- **NewsLink**: *http://newslink.org*
  Find newspapers, magazines, and radio/TV sites in the U.S. and around the world.

- **News Archives on the Web**: *http://metalab.unc.edu/slanews/internet/archives.html*
  The place to go to find newspaper archives and how to access them.

- **Electronic reproductions** of current editions of hundreds of newspapers from cover to cover are available from two providers: Newsstand at *www.newsstand.com* or Pressdisplay at *www.pressdisplay.com*.

- **Newseum's Interactive Museum of News**: *www.newseum.org/today-sfrontpages/flash*
  Browse through reproductions of daily front pages from newspapers around the world.

- **PubList.Com**: *www.publist.com*
  Information about 150,000 publications including Web address if there is one.

- **Many of the large search engines** provide a news aggregator service, where you can read up-to-the-minute news from hundreds of news providers in one place. For an example, check out *http://news.google.com*.

LIBRARIES

Libraries are found in universities, schools, government agencies, and associations. There are national, state, and local libraries. There are legal, medical, and business libraries. Although they are usually found within the sites of the sponsoring organization, some (like the Library of Congress) stand alone. Some don't even exist outside the Web, like the Internet Public Library (*www.ipl.org*). Library sites fill the mission of the library itself: to collect, organize, and facilitate the use of information. Libraries collect and provide access to information generated by all four of the information sources identified in Chapter 2: Informal, institutional, scholarly, and journalistic sources find their way into library collections.

Many public libraries in the U.S. use the Web address structure of: *www.lib.ci.****.**. us*, where **** is the city name, and ** is the two-letter state code; or *www.****.lib.**. us* where **** is the city or county name, and ** is the two-letter state code. For example, the Web address of the Hennepin County Library in Minnesota is *www. hennepin.lib.mn.us*. Others use the .org domain. Libraries affiliated with educational institutions will be found under the .edu domain.

Types of information they provide

Online catalogs of the library collection. Many have guides for how to use the Internet. Special resource guides. Access to databases. Local libraries will have area-specific information and resources. Some libraries provide access to digitally scanned materials from their print, audio, or video collections so users across the globe can have access to these resources.

Why they provide it

Libraries exist to organize and share information; Web sites are designed to do that.

Uses in reporting and research

- Find local and regional information on public library sites.

- Find experts by locating authors of books on a topic in online catalogs.

- Find librarians working in specialty libraries and use them as a resource for questions on a topic.

Tips and traps

- Some library sites are just informational pages about the library. Others are full of information and really have to be browsed. Take the time to get to know your local library resources.

- Some of the services available on library sites can only be used by library card-holders or, in the case of universities, by students or faculty.

Exercises for library sites

- Use one of the library finders listed below and locate a Web site for a library in your vicinity. Look the site over—what did you find you didn't expect to find?

- Find literacy programs in the Dallas area using the Dallas Public Library Community Information Database: *http://dallaslibrary.org*.

- You want to find a listing of all the mayors of Minneapolis over the years. Check the Hennepin County Public Library Fugitive Fact File: *www.hclib.org/pub/search/fff_public.cfm*.

- A candidate for public office in your state with the last name Poythress claims that her relatives were land-owners in the colony of Virginia as early as the 1750s. Use the Land Office Grants that have been digitally scanned from the collections of the Library of Virginia to check out her claim: *www.lva.lib.va.us/whatwehave/land/index.htm*

Finding library sites

- **LibWeb Library Servers** via WWW: *http://lists.webjunction.org/libweb*
  More than 7,400 pages from libraries in more than 125 countries.

- **State Libraries**: *www.publiclibraries.com/state_library.htm*
  Links to state libraries, presidential libraries, university and college libraries across the United States.

- **Use the directory** feature of one of the major search engines to locate libraries by type. For instance, the Yahoo! Search directory leads you to listings for 471 academic libraries at *http://dir.yahoo.com/Reference/Libraries/Academic_Libraries*.

These are just some of the kinds of creators of Web sites. Hospitals, law firms, police agencies, political parties, and churches are some of the other types of organizations which create Web sites. As you explore the Web and encounter Web sites from different types of sponsors, keep in mind who put the Web site together, why they have done it, what kind of information they provide, and how you might use it in your reporting and research. This consciousness about the usefulness of different types of Web sites will serve you well as you start learning how to efficiently and effectively use the Web for research.

WEB SEARCH SITES

Before we talk about the basics of searching, we need to talk about the types of Web search sites.

It seems there is a new Web search service announced every day. If you count the number of sites which compile directories or lists of links to Web sites, there would be tens of thousands of Web site finding aids.

Most of these search services are free to the user. They make their money through selling ads or offering additional premium services. Some charge Web site sponsors who want to be listed high up in the relevancy ranking.

Web search sites break down into a few general categories:

- **Directory search sites**

- **Indexed search sites**

- **Meta search sites**

- **Web rings**

- **The deep Web**

Within these categories, Web search sites can also be grouped according to the scope of their coverage. Some search sites are "omni guides" in that they incorporate information from a vast array of sources and subjects (e.g. Google, AltaVista, Teoma, Yahoo, Snap). Other search sites are devoted to a specific and defined subject area or a specific type of content (e.g. Findlaw, Envirolink, TotalNews, Google Image Search).

The lines between these categories can be pretty fuzzy. Some of the "omni" search sites include both directory and index features. Some of the search sites have licensed the software from seeming "competitors" to conduct their searches.

To understand search sites and how best to use them you need to know how a search engine gathers information about the Web pages and Web sites it includes.

Unless you are really motivated, it is almost impossible to learn the ins and outs of all of the major search services. Our advice is to think of search services like we think of friends. It is better to know and understand a few really well so you can depend on them rather than to know many but only superficially.

So go visit a number from each of the following categories, but select just a few you really want to get to know.

In this chapter we will look at the different types of Web search sites and finding aids and discuss their general characteristics. We will also look at the kinds of differences to look for between the sites that fall into that category. We will not try to profile individual sites. There are some great books and Web sites that do that (see "For more information" boxes). We will list 5 to 10 of the sites that fall into that category so you can make some visits and look them over yourself.

For each of the search site categories we'll look at:

- **What they are and how they are created:** An overview of the process for getting information about Web sites into this kind of service and how the service works.

- **When to use them:** A note about the usefulness of each particular type of search site for different research needs.

- **What you are searching in the system:** A brief description of the actual contents of the database you are searching on the site, and how much and what type of information there is on the entries about Web sites or pages in the database.

- **Strengths:** What is particularly good about this type of search site.

- **Weaknesses:** What to look out for when using this type of search site.

- **Other features commonly offered:** What else you can do on these kinds of sites.

- **Examples of sites:** Names and Web addresses of 5 to 10 of these types of sites.

- **Exercises:** A few sample questions to try your hand at using these types of sites. (Refer to the searching basics section of this chapter for more about searching.)

DIRECTORY SITES

In the beginning there was Yahoo! Begun in April 1994 by two Stanford electrical engineering students, David Filo and Jerry Yang, Yahoo!'s directory architecture was a way to track the interesting sites that were starting to be published on the World Wide Web. Yahoo! has since added an index feature, but it still serves as one of the premier directory sites (although you have to hunt around on the page to find the link to the directory section of the site).

What they are and how they are created

Directory search sites are subject-organized directories of Web sites. Search site administrators enter sites into the directory and assign hierarchical subject categories to the entries which then become part of the search site's database.

Some directory sites are "omni guides" because they cover the entire range of subjects represented on the Web. They are trying to index Web pages on aardvarks to Zulus and everything in between. Other directory sites are subject specific and focus on a narrow range of materials.

When to use them

When you are just looking for a sampling of good sites on general topics, for browsing or for specific topics in-depth. Don't use them if you are looking for very specific terms or people (unless the people are celebrities or well known).

What is in the database you are searching

You are searching on the subject terms used to describe the page or site, the title and address of the Web site, and, sometimes, a brief description of the contents of the site. They do not index every word on the site.

Some directory sites are more careful about evaluating the sites they include in their database than others. A very heavily-used search site such as Yahoo! allows users to submit content, meaning that the sites included in the database may not be particularly selective. Other directory sites are more carefully constructed by subject experts and can provide more selective guidance.

Strengths

- The careful categorization puts organizational structure to the indexing of the Web.

- With the more selective directory searches you are sent to higher quality sites.

- Some have ratings for sites in the directory based on different criteria.

- Some have annotations that describe the contents of the site so you can judge whether it is a good fit before you go there.

Weaknesses

- Very limited coverage of the Web's contents.

- Some directory sites are not willing to share information about how they select the sites they include in their database.

- General "omni" sites lack focus; they try to cover all topics.

- A Web site can be indexed under multiple subjects, so there can be duplication of results.

- Some directory sites are starting to charge Web sites for better placement in the results, so returns might be based on payola, not relevance.

Other features commonly offered

Many of these sites are becoming "portals"—doorways to all the features and functions of the Web. They will offer e-mail, ads, news, e-commerce links, and different subject "channels." Some also allow you to search their databases by specific type of information (video, images, etc.).

Examples of "omni guide" directory sites

- **InfoMine**: *http://infomine.ucr.edu*
  Built by academic librarians and aimed at scholarly research needs.

- **Librarians' Internet Index**: *http://lii.org*
  A general directory site with very clear selection criteria, compiled by librarians, and billed as "Websites you can trust."

- **Snap**: *www.snap.com*
  Offers a visual preview of results and suggests search terms and phrases.

- **World Wide Web Virtual Library**: *http://vlib.org*
  Claims to be the "oldest catalogue on the Web."

- **Directory portion of Yahoo!**: *http://dir.yahoo.com*

Exercises for directory sites

- Think of a fairly broad topic. Go to three of the "omni guide" directory sites listed above and browse through the subject listings for that topic. How do the subject categories used in the various sites differ?

- A Krishna temple is opening in town. Where can you go to find Web sites about Hare Krishna?

- You want information about violence in middle and high schools. Find relevant Web sites in Yahoo! by browsing through the subject categories.

Examples of subject-specific directory sites:

- **Envirolink**: *www.envirolink.org*
  Environmental information (find the directories at the bottom of the page)

- **FindLaw**: *www.findlaw.com*
  Legal information

- **Landings**: *www.landings.com*
  Aviation information (find the aviation directory at the bottom of the page)

- **Officer.com**: *www.officer.com*
  Law enforcement officer links

- **Medical Matrix**: *www.medmatrix.org*
  You have to register to use this site, which has a well organized collection of medical and health links.

- **TotalNews**: *www.totalnews.com*
  Select directories of news stories by topic (sports, entertainment, politics) or by source (ABC News, newspapers in Alabama, etc.).

Exercises for subject-specific directory sites

- You are working on a story about hazardous waste transportation issues. Look in Envirolink for resources, then look in one of the omni guides. Which one had more references? Which had more relevant sources? Which was easier to use?

- You have to cover the unveiling of a new memorial to police who have been killed in the line of duty. Where might you find some background information on other police memorials in the U.S.?

- Your city's airport press agents proudly announce the signing on of the 86th airline to bring service to their facility. In the press release it says, "This makes the number of airlines using our airport even larger than London's Heathrow." Are you just going to put that into the news story or are you going to check it out?

INDEXED SEARCH SITES

What they are and how they are created

Instead of relying on humans to organize the Web entries, indexed search sites rely on software, typically called "spiders." One of the clearest explanations of how spiders work comes from Danny Sullivan, the master reviewer of search engine technology. This comes from his excellent site Search Engine Watch: *www.searchenginewatch.com.*

> "Search engines have three major elements. First is the spider, also called the crawler. The spider visits a Web page, reads it, and then follows links to other pages within the site. This is what it means when someone refers to a site being "spidered" or "crawled." The spider returns to the site on a regular basis, such as every month or two, to look for changes.
>
> Everything the spider finds goes into the second part of a search engine, the index. The index, sometimes called the catalog, is like a giant book containing a copy of every Web page that the spider finds. If a Web page changes, then this book is updated with new information.
>
> Sometimes it can take a while for new pages or changes that the spider finds to be added to the index. Thus, a Web page may have been "spidered" but not yet "indexed." Until it is indexed—added to the index—it is not available to those searching with the search engine.
>
> Search engine software is the third part of a search engine. This is the program that sifts through the millions of pages recorded in the index to find matches to a search and rank them in order of what it believes is most relevant." (Copyright 1999 internet.com LLC. All Rights Reserved. Used with Permission.)

As with directory sites, index search sites can be comprehensive "omni" sites or they can be highly specialized and dedicated to one particular topic.

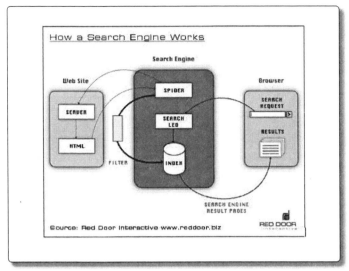

www.imediaconnection.com/images/content/chart_060320_redDoor.gif

How much of the Web they index
and their turn-around time

Spiders can only index the "surface" Web. Much of the content of the "deep" Web (see page 132) cannot be indexed, so no Web search site is comprehensive. That said, the number of Web sites that are "spidered" is staggering and as the technology improves, the accuracy and precision of indexed searches also gets better.

How often the spider is sent out to capture information to add to the index varies from one search site to another. It can be as often as every few weeks or as infrequently as several months or more.

What is in the system you are searching

The spider captures every page and the indexing software indexes every word on the page (except for so-called "stop words," common words like "the," "and," "a"— different search engines have different sets of stop words). The Web address, Web page title, and "meta-tags" are also indexed. Meta-tags are words added to the keywords and descriptions of the site that can be read by the indexing software but which aren't seen on the Web page itself. This is why you sometimes get sites, usually porn sites, that don't match what you are searching. The Web page creator throws all kinds of words into the meta-tags hoping people searching on one of the words will get their Web site in the results.

Some search engines don't actually index every word on the page; they may just do the first dozen or so lines. It is important to read the documentation if you are interested in understanding the workings of a particular search engine.

Strengths

- The thoroughness of the indexing. Much of the page is indexed instead of just a description.

- The coverage of the Web—a larger slice of the Web's contents are indexed.

- The ability to find specific words and names located deep within a Web page.

- The relevancy ranking feature of most of the search engines brings the best of the results to the top.

- The more sophisticated index sites also organize search results according to "peer ranking" (giving you results based on the number of links from the largest number of pages also ranked high by the service) or "bundling" of results based on concepts, domains, or other features.

Weaknesses

- The good, bad, and the ugly of the Web are all mixed together in the database—there is no quality control.

- The results list is sometimes overwhelming, because there are so many hits.

- The index can be out of date; items you click to from the results list may no longer be on the Web.

- Going from one indexed search site to another can be confusing, because they use different commands and have different features.

- Many of them offer so many other features that it is hard to find the basic search functions within the search site's page.

When to use them

- If you are going for a specific rather than a broad topic. For broad topics, finding sites under subject categories in a human-indexed directory might be better.

- If a search in a human-indexed directory did not find anything.

- If you are going for a more comprehensive search and want to find a lot of the available resources on that topic.

- If you want to search for particular file types (PowerPoint presentations, pdf files), languages, or domain types (just .edu sites or just .org sites).

Other features commonly offered

Many index search sites are also offering Yahoo-like directories of Web sites with much more selective lists of Web sites on a topic. Many will have searches of other Internet functions available in addition to the Web page search; they will have newsgroup message searches or blog searches, for example. Most have shopping "channels" and other transaction features.

Examples of indexed sites

- **Google**: *www.google.com*
  A search site so popular its name has been adopted as a verb: "I'll google it and see what turns up." Google has a large number of search features and capabilities plus news, shopping, mapping, and many other services.

- **AltaVista**: *www.altavista.com*
  Claims to have invented the first full-text searchable database on the Web in 1995. Allows for very precise searches.

- **Ask**: *www.ask.com*
  Formerly known as "Ask Jeeves."

- **Snap**: *www.snap.com*
  In addition to using traditional spider technology, Snap also uses click-stream information from a network of one million Internet users. The system records and processes which Web sites users spend time on, and which sites they quickly leave, so you may have better luck finding just what you are looking for.

Exercises for indexed sites

- You are going to be interviewing a world-renowned cytologist. You must have missed class the day they talked about that in school and aren't really sure what a cytologist does. Where can you find some information about cytology and come up with some good questions to ask her?

- You are looking for the text of the Universal Human Rights bill, or something like that. You aren't sure of the exact name of it. Can you find it? It's pretty old, from the 40s or 50s and it was some kind of United Nations thing.

- Do a search on your state or country. You get so many hits you want to narrow it down. Find Web pages that mention your state and crime.

- You sometimes get these strange messages when you click to a site on a set of results, stuff like "404 Not Found," or "Connection Refused by Host." Find a listing and explanation of Internet error messages.

- Does anyone sell manure on the Web (no, real manure, from farm animals)?

Examples of subject-specific index sites

- **LawCrawler**: *http://lawcrawler.findlaw.com*
  Specific spiders sent out to international, U.S. federal, and specific state law and government sites. Uses Google search engine technology.

- **MP3 Downloads**: *www.mp3.com*
  A search engine for locating electronic music files, especially useful if you are looking for content for your multimedia Web site.

- **Healthfinder**: *www.healthfinder.gov/search*
  A service of the National Health Information Center which combines an index search feature with directory-type information.

- **Business Publications Search Index**: *www.bpubs.com*
  Another combination index/directory search tool

- **TotalNews**: *www.totalnews.com*
  Searches through news Web sites and brings you current news that hits the subject you search.

- **Government Information**: *www.searchgov.com*
  Federal, state, and local government information from the legislative and executive branches. Uses Google search engine to search .gov domain sites.

- **Blogs**: *www.technorati.com*
  A site that includes both an index search feature and a directory of blogs by subject matter.

Exercises for subject-specific index sites

- You get a tip that a legislator in your state who had been arrested and convicted a few years back had his record expunged. Where can you find information about what expunging a record means?

- You're doing a series on gun control and you just want to keep up with what kinds of stories other news organizations have been doing on it. Where could you go to find some recent stories on gun control?

- There's a news release about radon levels in the air and water in your region. You've got the environmental information, but you need to know more about the health effects. Find some medical sites with information about radon.

- You want to know how states have been implementing the federal "No Child Left Behind" legislation. Find some state sites that detail activities.

META-SEARCH SITES

What they are and how they are created

Think of meta-search sites as one-stop search sites. They don't create their own indexes of information about Web pages. They send out the search you put into the meta-search site and submit it to all the other search sites which then search their own indexes and send back the results. You'll get a compilation of the results coming from the different search sites.

How much of the Web they index and their turn-around time

Because they combine the results from a number of different index and directory search sites, a meta-search is probably one of the most comprehensive searches. It is still not covering the whole Web, but it may snag things collectively that you wouldn't have gotten from individual search sites.

What is in the system you are searching

The search contents will be the same as for the index or directory search, but the meta-search site will usually impose a cut-off determined by the number of documents retrieved.

Strengths

- Enter one search and get results back from multiple search sites, usually with duplicate results eliminated automatically.

- Gets the best results from the different search sites quickly and easily.

Weaknesses

- Some major search sites aren't available on meta-search pages.

- Searches can time out if the search site the search is sent to doesn't respond quickly. It will come back saying there were no results, but that doesn't mean there is nothing on that topic at the site.

- The search refinement features (like phrase searching or boolean connectors) are often stripped in the translation to different search sites. Searching is less precise than going to the individual sites and searching.

When to use them

When you've got a specific obscure topic and want to fling the net out widely. Also useful for doing a broad search and scanning the top results from a variety of search sites.

Other features commonly offered

They often will search other databases other than just Web pages (newsgroup messages, blogs, pdf files, newswires, etc.).

Examples of meta-search sites

- **Dogpile**: *www.dogpile.com*
  Has a "Comparison View" feature that lets you compare results from the leading engines with the click of a button.

- **Ixquick**: *www.ixquick.com*
  Results are awarded one star for every search engine that chooses it as one of the ten best results, so five-star results are more accurate.

- **Search**: *www.search.com*
  Allows for specialty searches by subject categories.

- **SurfWax**: *www.surfwax.com*
  Allows you to capture, store, and organize your research.

Exercise for meta-search sites

- Try some of the searches you did in other exercises in the meta-search engines. What did you find that you didn't get before?

WEB RINGS

What they are and how they are created

Web rings are affiliations of related types of Web sites. They are, in some ways, like a consortium of Web sites on related topics. They support each other by providing links from one site to the next in the Web ring.

How much of the Web they index and their turn-around time

They don't index Web sites; they link Web sites.

What is in the system you are searching

The main Web ring search site (*www.webring.org*) has descriptions of the Web rings with links to each site.

Strengths

- You'll often find the more esoteric and fringe types of sites affiliated here, the ones that might not get noticed by the big search site indexes.

- It's easy to hop around from one site to the next to get a sense of the information they have.

- Many support group and personal page sites link together in Web rings. These can be a good way to find informal sources through personal story pages, created by people with experience (but not necessarily expertise) on a wide variety of activities, hobbies, etc.

- Each Webring.org site is managed by a "RingMaster" who is responsible for maintaining the quality of the ring and for enforcing terms of inclusion.

Weaknesses

- You can't search the contents of the pages on the Web rings, just the descriptions of the ring.

- You can't really tell what site will be next in the chain when you click on the Web ring label.

- Most of the sites on Web rings are personal pages, coming from individuals who can, and do, say anything. Use content from these sites with caution and follow up by traditional reporting techniques (i.e. call them and interview them and then check out what they say).

When to use them

When you want to identify informal sources that might add color to a story. When you are wandering and want to find a number of similar sites easily. These rings make it easy to travel from one to the next.

How to find Web rings

WebRing (*www.webring.org*) offers a subject directory and a searchable database of Web ring descriptions. Search a topic, click on one of the Web ring names, and get a list of all the Web sites on the ring.

Exercises for Web rings

- You are doing a story about a child with neurofibromatosis. You want to see if others have been through a situation similar to what this family has been through. Find some personal pages of neurofibromatosis sufferers.

- There is going to be a James Dean film festival next weekend. You want to interview some fans of the long-dead movie star. Can you find any Dean fanatics?

THE DEEP WEB

Even the largest of the search sites on the Web include less than a quarter of the Web's contents. Here is what is not indexed or searchable through Web search sites:

- Content in sites requiring a log in: Most Web indexing can't get behind a registration screen so, for example, content on the *New York Times* Web site won't be indexed.

- Some content in frames and image maps: Some of the formatting techniques on Web pages will make indexing impossible.

- CGI and ASP output: CGI (Common Gateway Interface) and ASP (Active Server Pages) are ways Web sites create pages on the fly. Since these are dynamically created the pages cannot be indexed and found in a Web site search.

- Content in databases on the Web site: There might be a wonderful database on a Web site but you won't find what is actually in it through a Web search.

- Intranet pages: Pages that sit behind a "firewall" on a corporate server aren't indexed.

- Sites with robots.txt files to keep files off limits: Web page designers can add a code to certain pages or files they don't want Web search site indexing to pick up.

DEEP WEB SEARCH SITES

What they are and how they are created

Most deep Web search sites are actually easily accessible. They are typically maintained by humans rather than by software and can take the form of index or directory-type search sites. In addition, deep Web content is available on some of the general search engine sites such as Google by using the features that allow you to search for specific formats of material such as news, video, images, etc.

When to use them

More and more useful information is stored in databases rather than as a static Web page, so if you are looking for information from a phone book, for instance, one of the deep Web search tools might work best. If you are looking for highly current, dynamically-changing information such as job listings, airline schedules, and similar data, you will want to use these tools. Also, you will find non-textual files such as music, images, video, and other new digital formats by using these tools rather than some of the more general search sites.

What is in the system you are searching

Much directory-type information is part of the deep Web. A few examples include:

- phone books

- "people finders" such as lists of professionals such as doctors or lawyers

- patents

- laws

- dictionary definitions

- items for sale in a Web store or on Web-based auctions

- digital exhibits

- multimedia and graph files

Late breaking items will also best be located on the deep Web. These include:

- news

- job postings

- available airline flights, hotel rooms, etc.

- stock and bond prices, market averages, etc.

Strengths

- This information is not accessible through the more general search sites. Therefore, you will find materials that will not show up using any other search method.

- More and more information is made accessible online through deep Web sites with features that block the general search tools. Some of the most valuable new content is going to be available this way.

Weaknesses

- Many deep Web sites are intended for subject specialists or those with a subscription to the service, so you need to allow enough time to gain access and understand what you've found.

- It may be difficult to determine the source of information in some of the deep Web sites you find. The notion of "scope notes" may be missing.

Other features commonly offered

Some deep Web sites include links to experts, authorities, or associations that specialize in the subject matter covered by the site.

Examples of deep Web search sites

- **BrightPlanet's CompletePlanet**: *www.completeplanet.com*
  Includes 70,000+ searchable databases and specialty search engines arranged in a directory search engine.

- **Search-22**: *www.search-22.com*
  A directory of thousands of specialty search engines, many of which provide access to information from the deep Web.

Exercises for deep Web searches

- After a large methamphetamine bust in your town, the local police announce a special training program for officers who work on the drug task force. Some local critics say the training program will be ineffective. How can you find information about similar programs elsewhere that can provide your audience with some opportunities for comparison?

- Try some of the searches you did in other exercises in the deep Web search engines. What did you find that you didn't get before?

FOR MORE INFORMATION

Books:

Dornfest, Rael, and Tara Calishain. *Google Hacks: Tips & Tools for Smarter Searching*. 2nd ed. Sebastopol, CA: O'Reilly Media, 2004.

Price, Gary. *The Extreme Searcher's Internet Handbook: A Guide for the Serious Searcher*. Medford, NJ: Cyberage Books/Information Today, Inc., 2004.

Schlein, Alan. *Find It Online: The Complete Guide to Online Research*. 4th ed. Lanham, MD: Facts on Demand Press, 2004

Newsletters:

The CyberSkeptics Guide to Internet Research
Evaluates important sites and strategies to help you use the Internet as a serious and cost-effective tool for research. Geared toward business research, market research, and competitive intelligence. 10 issues per year.
$164.95/year ($112.95/year for personal or nonprofit use)
www.cyberskeptic.com/cs

"Knowledge is of two kinds;
we know a subject ourselves,
or we know where we can
find information upon it."
— Samuel Johnson, 1775

WEB SEARCHING BASICS

As the previous chapter discussed, the World Wide Web is just one part of the information and communications functions enabled by the Internet. The different search sites on the Web are crucial in helping you locate valuable content from Web pages, newsgroups, and other parts of Internet accessible information.

Now that you are familiar with the different types of search sites on the Web, we should go over the basics of searching these sites. The following section will discuss:

- Focusing the search

- Search engine basics

- Search functions

- Search troubleshooting

- What search sites won't find

FOCUSING THE SEARCH

Look back at the Chapter 1 sections on defining the task and framing the question. As you start using search sites, remember how to focus on the task you need to accomplish and how to be clear about the question you need to answer. This will help you identify the type of search site you should use for specific types of tasks.

SEARCH ENGINE BASICS

The first thing you should do when you go to an unfamiliar search site (or even one you've been using, but with some degree of frustration) is to find the search help file. This is sometimes a challenge. The terms they use on different sites for the help file vary and are sometimes not very prominently displayed.

There are three main differences between the Web search sites and the traditional archive databases (like Dialog or LexisNexis):

- **Structured search vs natural language:** Dialog and LexisNexis searches are fairly rigidly constructed; you have to follow the right search syntax. For example, you might search for: *(car or auto or automotive or automobile) and insurance.*

  Web searches are natural language queries. You can type in the words any way you want, even as a sentence, "*I want to find stuff about automobile insurance.*" You can do more structured kinds of searches on Web search sites, but they are designed as natural language search engines.

- **Word match vs fuzzy logic:** Traditional database searches retrieve only those documents which match exactly the terms you typed in. Something is either a true match or it is not.

  Web searches use "fuzzy logic"; they are not so black or white. They will find exact matches but they'll also retrieve words that are pretty darn close to what you asked for or they might prompt you with alternative spellings as with Google's "Did you mean…" message at the top of the results page.

- **Chronological display vs relevancy ranking:** Traditional database searches rank their results in either chronological or reverse chronological order (oldest to newest or newest to oldest).

  The default display for most Web search sites is relevancy, not date (although some do have an option for reverse chronological order display). In relevancy ranked results displayed first will be those pages with the greatest occurrence of the terms you've asked for, or the most prominent location of those terms on the page (in the title or Web address or lead paragraph). The "fuzzy" logic search is why you get so many results in Web site searches; some don't seem to have the words you've looked for. But the relevancy ranking is why the best material for your search is at the top of the list. Even though you get 245,865 hits on a search, you'll often find the first 10 or so are the most relevant.

While all search sites use relevancy ranking to sort results, you need to know that these sites also generate revenue by allowing Web site sponsors to pay for a high ranking. The paying sponsors choose the search words that potential Web surfers might use and pay to ensure that their sites come up in a top spot when those words are used in the search. The paid listings are typically labeled in some way that alerts you that the site sponsors have paid for that high ranking. The paid listings may be segregated to a particular area of the search screen (the right sidebar, for instance) or say "sponsored link" or other similar label.

Another thing to be aware of with Web search sites is that some of them actually use the same search software. Knowing which software is used can help because once you know the search functions on one search site you can be pretty sure you'll know how to use the other sites that use that software.

One of the most important things to remember is that the search site is going to look for the word you typed, not necessarily the word you mean. It's looking for matching characters, not a matching definition. You're looking for Matisse, the artist, but when you type in "Matisse" you get a software company, a restaurant and other unrelated Matisses. You'll want to get specific in your search (put in his first name, too).

SEARCH FUNCTIONS

Let's look at six basic search functions and how they operate in Web search sites. There are dozens of search services on the Web. For each of the following functions we will profile how some of the major services use these features:

- Boolean logic

- Proximity searching

- Truncation

- Field searching

- Date range searching

- File type searching

For specifics about how each of these operate (or don't operate) in various search sites be sure to read the site's help files. Every search site has a section for "advanced" searches. Most of these features require you to use the "advanced" section of the search site. (Also, see "For more information" for books and Web sites with more detail about Web searching.)

Boolean logic: And, Or, Not

The logic of Boolean algebra, named for a British mathematician named George Boole (1815-1864), refers, according to Encyclopedia Britannica (*www.britannica. com*), to the "symbolic system of mathematical logic that represents relationships between entities—either ideas or objects." When used in the context of database searching, it is a way to represent the relationship between search terms.

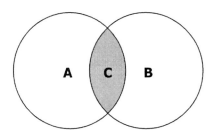

There are three logical connectors between search terms: AND, OR, NOT. They are frequently described using a visual representation of the relationship between the terms using overlapping circles, called a Venn diagram.

AND: The AND relationship between search terms would be represented as two overlapping circles. If your search terms were *poodles* (A) and *breeding* (B), using AND, the retrieved documents would include *both* of those terms. The overlapping part of the circles labeled C in this diagram is the AND set.

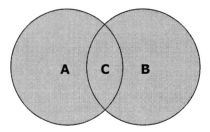

OR: The OR relationship between search terms would be represented as everything in both of the overlapping circles of the Venn diagram.

If you did a search using the term *Medicare* (A) OR *Medicaid* (B), you would get entries represented by everything in A, B, and C (with C being documents that have both terms, *Medicare* and *Medicaid*, in them). The OR search is the most inclusive of the logical connectors.

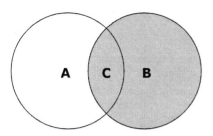

NOT: NOT is the most dangerous of the Boolean connectors to use. You can inadvertently leave out relevant hits because they happen to contain the word you "NOT" out.

For example, you want to see if there is anything written about a guy named Dave Matthews, but not the Dave Matthews of the Dave Matthews Band. So you search for *"Dave Matthews"* (A) *NOT band* (B). The results will be the part represented by the A. The trouble with the search is that it will knock out any articles that said *band*, including a great article on Dave Matthews, the guy you are looking for, which happens to say "He played in the high school band." NOT is usually not a good searching route to take (unless it is to NOT out articles from a particular publication or if it is used in a field search—see below).

Web search sites usually have two levels of searching. The level you see on the home page is usually the "simple" search. In almost all instances, the "simple" search uses the Boolean AND strategy when you type in search terms. That is, the search engine will retrieve items that include all of the terms you have requested. If you want to take advantage of the more precise searching using Boolean connectors you have to go to the "advanced" search.

Most Web search sites don't use the Boolean connector language of AND, OR, NOT. Instead, when you go to the "advanced search" page you will have several choices that implicitly use Boolean logic. For example, the "advanced search" choices in Google offer you the option to find results "with all of the words," the equivalent of the Boolean operator AND. Or you can choose to find results "with at least one of the words," which is the equivalent of the Boolean operator OR. Or you can choose to find results "without the words," the Boolean equivalent of NOT.

Other Web search sites will have similar "advanced search" options, perhaps worded slightly differently. But if you understand the underlying logic of Boolean operators, you will be able to decipher the choices and make the right one for your search.

One of the problems with many Web search sites is the inability to "nest" search terms. For example, you might want to set up multiple OR sets: *(money OR dollars OR currency) and (saving OR investing OR hoarding)*. These elaborate search relationships that can be used in the big commercial database services are usually not seen in Web search sites.

FOR MORE INFORMATION

Boolean Searching on the Internet: A Primer in Boolean Logic
www.internettutorials.net/boolean.html

Proximity searching: "phrase searching"

Proximity is the search function that lets you determine the closeness of search terms to each other. If you do a phrase search or have search terms appear near to each other, you are doing a proximity search. In commercial database services, proximity searching can be quite elaborate. You can ask for a word to be within 5 or 10 or even 38 words of another word or within the same paragraph. In Web search services, however, there are fewer options.

Of all the proximity functions, the phrase search is the one available on almost every Web search site. It is also the one that is most consistent in how you designate it across all the different search engines; Use quotation marks around the terms you want to search as a phrase.

If you are searching for a phrase, do not forget to use the quotes. If you are covering an art house revival of Salvador Dali's film "Andalusian Dog" and want some background, typing in *andalusian dog* in Ask will return 46,000 hits (the default search when you just type in terms is an AND search).

Typing in *"andalusian dog"* (in quotation marks) will get you 3,600 hits, still a large number but much more manageable, and relevant, than the results without the quotation marks.

Truncation: rank ranked ranking ranker ranks

Sometimes you want to search a term by various possible endings or variations of the word. There are two different types:

- **Word endings:** Put in the word stem and truncation symbol and the search will fill in the possible endings. This is called "forward" truncation. Most of the services that have truncation use an asterisk (*) for the truncation symbol. Others do some automatic pluralization (put in a noun and it will automatically look for the plural). Others don't do truncation.

- **Wildcard:** Type in the word with an asterisk (*) in spaces where you want words with any letters in that position to be retrieved. Wildcard searches are useful if you aren't sure how a word is spelled. Is it Johannesburg or Johanesberg or Johanesburg? Search *Johan*esb*rg.*

TIP: Be thoughtful when using truncation. If you search for *horse**, you'll get *horse* and *horses* and *horse's*, of course, but you'll also get *horseshoe, horsefly, horseshow, horseman,* etc. It might be better to just do an OR search and string together the various words you really want searched.

Field searching: title:"how to do field searching"

Field searching may be the most useful way to narrow and focus your searching. When you do a field search you are looking for the search term to appear in a particular part of the retrieved page. Different search services offer different types of field searches; check their help files, but here are two of the most useful fields to use in searching:

- **Title:** A title field search will only retrieve pages with your search term in the title of the page. This is useful for broad searches. Relevant documents would probably have the term you are searching for in the title. Looking for background about coal mining? In Google search *"coal mining"* and get 717,100 hits, but search *title: "coal mining"* and get 24 hits.

- **Domain or URL:** A Web address (URL) search is a great way to narrow down the search to particular types of sites. If you know that a government agency would be the best, most reliable source for information you are seeking, narrow the search to just .gov sites. If you think an association would be the likeliest source, search in the .org domain. You need material about fire survival techniques and don't want to get every commercial page selling fire alarms, you just want information from organizations concerned with fire safety. In AltaVista search for *"fire survival"* and combine it with the "by domain" feature in advanced search using *domain:org* and get 208 hits, whereas *"fire survival"* retrieves 53,900 pages.

Date range searching

Date searching is one of the staples of commercial database searching. It is a way to get articles from certain time periods or since a certain date. On the Web, date searching is more problematic. It's hard to know if the date being searched is when the information was originally published, when it went onto the Web site, or is just the date of the search site's indexing of that page. In most cases it is the later, which is actually the least relevant date for researchers.

The way date searching is done on the search sites that provide it is very different, and difficult to describe. It's best to read the help files on the search site you are using to see if date range searching is an option.

File type searching: filetype:doc

As we've said, the Web now provides access to many types of file content beyond Web pages, including materials created using Word, PostScript or WordPerfect word processing software; the content of someone's PowerPoint presentation or Excel spreadsheet; or documents stored electronically in Adobe's PDF (portable document format) file format.

A number of search sites allow you to specify the type of content you want to retrieve. For instance, if you are looking for the PowerPoint slides used by NASA's global warming expert James Hansen in the talk you covered last week, you could conduct a search in Google using the terms *"James Hansen"* and *filetype:ppt* and retrieve those slides if he had posted them on the Web.

SEARCH TROUBLESHOOTING

- **Too many results:** Although the relevancy ranking feature of Web search software will probably pull the most relevant results to the top of the list, it is disconcerting to get 14,000,003 hits when you do a search. If this happens, think of ways to narrow. Is there a specific domain you'd want to search? Is there a word you can AND into the search to narrow it down? Use the "Search within results" box at the bottom of Google's search results page and add an additional term to further refine your search.

- **Too few results:** If you get few or no results, check your searching syntax. You may have put a space in where it wasn't needed (in a field search, for example). Check your spelling; you may need to do a wildcard search to get alternate spellings.

- **Get a good result, but can't get the page:** There is often a considerable interval between the times when a search site's content is scanned. Consequently, a page which was found the last time the search software scanned that site might have moved or been deleted but the reference to it in the database is still there. When the search site lists a page but you get a "page can't be found" error when you click on the link, you may be able to use the "cached" feature if you are using Google. Google allows you to retrieve the last version of the page that was functioning by clicking on "Cached" next to the URL. You need to be careful about using possibly outdated information from a cached site, but it may be the only way to recover material that has otherwise disappeared.

WHAT SEARCH SITES WON'T FIND—THE DEEP WEB

As our earlier discussion of the deep Web indicated, even the largest of the search sites on the Web index less than a quarter of the Web's contents. Database content, certain types of information formats, information behind a firewall, or sites with spider blockers won't be included in the search sites we've discussed.

"The modern age has a false sense of security because of the great mass of data at its disposal. But the valid issue is the extent to which man knows how to form and master the material at his command." — Johann Wolfgang von Goethe, 1832

FOR MORE INFORMATION

Best Search Tools Chart
http://infopeople.org/search/chart.html

Search Engine Watch
Everything you'd want to know about search engines
www.searchenginewatch.com

Search Engine News
Author Tara Calishain's Web site
for updates about search engine developments.
www.researchbuzz.org/wp

Calishain, Tara. *Web Search Garage*.
Upper Saddle River, NJ: Prentice Hall PTR, 2004.

WHAT'S NEXT

As the Web develops and grows into a more and more sophisticated information searching and retrieval tool, the ways we interact with Web content will change. While we are still a bit away from data orchestration scene from *Minority Report*, we are moving into increasingly interesting information visualization. Searches which show the relevance of a particular story in relation to others or which provide intuitive links to related content are being developed. An interesting example is C/Net's (*www.cnet.com*) "Big Picture" feature, wherein the story you are reading is placed in a "visual map" of related stories and content. This type of visual contextualization is going to be an exciting part of the next wave of Web development.

Chapter 4

Types of Material Online:
Comparisons of Commercial
Services and Web Sites

So far, most of this guide has been talking about the Internet and, more specifically, the World Wide Web. This is appropriate since the Web has become the information utility most available to and used by journalists and researchers.

But we need to talk about commercial services, too. Text archives and public records databases for which you need a subscription are bread-and-butter resources for information professionals and news researchers. Although many of these resources have migrated to Web-based interfaces (you don't need to dial out to their computer—you can go through the Internet), they are a somewhat different breed than the Web sites we've been talking about.

The first shots of the information revolution came from commercial database services. Defined as "a collection of data or body of information that is organized for rapid retrieval via a computer," databases have been the foundation of computer-assisted research since the late 1970s.

Commercial database services act as agents for the individual databases developed by database producers (such as government agencies, newspapers, magazines, and associations). They are the vendors of the data to the public, offering computer space, search software, marketing, and access in exchange for part of the revenue generated by people using the database.

In the age of the Web, many of these database producers have cut out the commercial vendor "middle-man." They are selling access to their archives and databases directly to the information consumer on their Web sites.

This is good news because the cost of database searching is usually considerably cheaper through the producer's Web site than through a commercial "re-seller." The bad news, though, is the loss of the convenience of one-stop searching. On commercial services one search hits lots of files. There are some Web search sites that are trying to provide that sort of service but with limited success.

In this chapter we will discuss the different types of material that can be found in commercial databases and compare these services to Web resources that retrieve the same types of materials. For the most part, the commercial services we will discuss are the "Big Four" text archives—Dialog, LexisNexis, Newsbank, and Factiva—and public records databases.

Many university and public libraries are making available access to the commercial databases they subscribe to through their Web sites. Usually, however, this service is only available to registered users (students, faculty, or library card holders).

Here are the types of information available on commercial database services, how they compare with Web-based access to these materials, and how they can be used in newsroom research and reporting. Individual databases consist of one or more of the following types of information:

- **Bibliographic citations and abstracts**

- **Articles and transcripts**

- **Books and directories**

- **Government documents**

- **Public records**

- **Consumer records**

- **Multimedia: photos, graphics, audio, and video**

FOR MORE INFORMATION

Gale Directory of Databases. Annual Edition.
Farmington Hills, MI: Thomson/Gale Group.
Profiles thousands of databases from around the world.
Find information at The Gale Group: *www.gale.com.*

Information Today: the newspaper for information professionals
Searcher: the magazine for database professionals
Online: the leading magazine for information professionals
Find information about these three magazines
and selected articles from past issues at *www.infotoday.com.*

First, a word about the cost of commercial databases

Commercial database vendors on and off the Web have been scrambling to figure out ways to keep their services competitive. Many services which were transactional cost-based (you paid for the amount of time you were online) are going to a flat-rate subscription. Some let you search for free but you pay per article you want to read. Others charge a different fee for the retrieval of different kinds of documents (particularly true with public records). These payment options, and the variety of sources available for finding the same kind of information, make careful shopping for information even more important.

BIBLIOGRAPHIC CITATIONS AND ABSTRACTS

The first databases available commercially were citation- or abstract-based. These databases provide references to articles available in thousands of publications. Bibliographic citations give only author, title, and publication information, while abstract citations also give a synopsis of the contents of the article. Most of these databases use a set of keywords or controlled vocabulary terms to aid in searching. Most producers of citation or abstract databases focus on a particular subject area. These databases do not include the full text of the items you find, so they can be great leads but you need to take a second step to find the entire article.

Examples of citation and abstract databases

- **Compendex:** Indexes scholarly and technical periodicals, conference proceedings, and report literature in all engineering disciplines including applied physics, electronics, materials science, and related fields in science and management from 1884 to the present.

- **Dissertation Abstracts:** More than 1.1 million citations to doctoral dissertations from accredited educational institutions back to 1861. Great for finding experts on esoteric topics.

- **PsycINFO:** Provides citations to the scholarly literature in the behavioral sciences and mental health back to 1887.

- **Social SciSearch:** The Institute for Scientific Information has pulled together these cites from 1,500 social science journals since 1972.

Uses in reporting and research

- Oldest material: Citation and abstract databases have references to material dating back the furthest. If you want to find a magazine article from the 1960s, you will most likely find a reference to it in a citation database.

- Esoteric material: Articles in obscure, scholarly, or special interest magazines are often indexed.

- Background information: The abstracts often give you basic information about the topic and lead you to alternative terms to search by.

- Locate experts: Authors of articles on specific topics can be great sources. Usually the magazine they wrote for can help you locate the writer.

- Story ideas: Just reading through a list of article titles can give you ideas and angles to the topic you may not have thought to pursue.

- Facts, statistics: Abstracts from some databases pull the most relevant facts and figures from the article, obviating the need to go to the source article.

Advantages of citation and abstract databases

- One-search access to information on millions of articles in thousands of journals.

- Locate subject specialists by finding authors of articles on specific topics.

- International coverage of topics of the most arcane and specific nature.

- Generally well-indexed with subject headings that make searching easier.

- Widest range of dates, usually indexes material dating much further back than full-text databases or material on the Web.

- Data are compiled by associations, institutes, and organizations that can be contacted for specific help in locating material.

Disadvantages and cautions

- It can be frustrating to find the perfect article but then not be able to get the full text easily.

- There are so many citations that it is easy to be overwhelmed with your search results unless you clearly target your search request.

- These are labor intensive databases; generating abstracts takes time, and there is often a considerable time lag in the posting of information. Citation and abstract databases will not give you quick access to the most current articles.

- Be sure to check whether the database is still active. Some databases are not being added to, but they continue to be searchable.

Finding citation and abstract databases

Commercial services

- **Dialog**: *www.dialog.com*
  Claims that it provides "more than 4 terabytes of content from the world's most authoritative publishers."

On the Web

- **ISI Web of Knowledge**: *http://isiwebofknowledge.com*
  More than 100 years of backfile records and cited references to a wide variety of scholarly literature.

- **Agricola**: *http://agricola.nal.usda.gov*
  The database of the National Agricultural Library (U.S. Dept. of Agriculture) that provides citations to agricultural information.

Search example

- After watching a TV movie about transporting nuclear waste, you decide to do a story and you want some background.

Searching in ISI Web of Knowledge using the terms "nuclear waste" and "transportation," you get this citation:

Title: Performance assessment of a nuclear waste repository
Author(s): Blum P, Mackay R, Riley MS, Knight JL
Source: INTERNATIONAL JOURNAL OF ROCK MECHANICS AND MINING SCIENCES 42 (5-6): 781-792 JUL-SEP 2005

- Another outbreak of gypsy moths is threatening your area's agricultural economy. You want to provide some information about the problem for your audience.

Searching in Agricola using "gypsy moths," you get this citation:

Title: The cost of slowing the spread of gypsy moth
Authors: Mayo, J.H., Straka, T.J., Leonard, D.S.
Source: Journal of economic entomology. 2003 Oct., v. 96, no. 5 p. 1448-1454.

ARTICLES AND TRANSCRIPTS

Also referred to as "full-text" databases, article and transcript databases take you a step further than the citation or abstract database by providing you with the complete text of articles, programs, speeches, and press releases. Most databases created since the mid-1980s provide full-text retrieval of material. Some full-text databases contain the text from just one publication; others are compilations of articles from a variety of source publications. Most commercial database services allow you to search for articles across a number of databases with one search, essentially making one huge compilation database from a number of separate databases.

Newspaper archives, which had been available exclusively through commercial database services, are now selling their archives on the Web. Some newspapers, not considered big enough to be included in the major commercial services, are providing online access to their archives for the first time through their Web sites.

There are a couple of services that try to facilitate cross-archive searching on the Web (see below).

Examples of article and transcript databases

- **AP, ITAR/TASS, Reuters, Xinhua, States News Services,** and other wire services

- **Business and Financial Library (LexisNexis)** offers thousands of articles from newspapers, magazines, financial analysts' reports, and topical reports.

- *Washington Post, El Pais, Jerusalem Post, Palm Beach Post*, and more than 500 other daily newspapers around the world

- **Screen Digest, Food Chemical News, Infectious Disease Weekly** and more than 4000 other newsletters and journals

- **20/20, 48 Hours, 60 Minutes** and more than 120 other news programs from ABC, CBC, CBS, NBC, CNN, FOX, NPR, and PBS

Uses in reporting and research

- **Background:** Full-text databases of news stories can help track down previous incidents, find background on the people involved in an incident, and otherwise put a news story into context. The broad range of publications, and their particular focus, offers articles representing a variety of viewpoints.

- **Scope and range:** The range of sources available in full-text databases make it possible to put a broader perspective on a local story, or to make an international story relevant to your community.

- **Facts, statistics:** Full-text articles from subject-specialty magazines and newsletters can reveal information from reports and studies that may not have gotten into mainstream publications.

- **Story ideas:** As with abstract databases, the articles retrieved can give you ideas about angles to follow in covering your story.

Advantages of full-text and transcript databases

- **Instant gratification:** You get the whole article immediately.

- **Online library:** You have the text of thousands of magazines, newspapers, speeches, and news programs instantly available.

- **Cost effective:** If you add up what paper subscriptions to these publications would cost, it may be cheaper to just access when you need them. Now with full-text archives on the Web, the cost has gotten even lower.

- **International scope:** Wire services and newspapers from around the world are available.

- **Regional information:** Access to a wide range of local newspapers and weekly magazines gives you a regional perspective on people and events.

Disadvantages and cautions

- **Difficult to search:** There is so much material that it is easy to retrieve too many articles.

- **Difficult to search (part 2):** There are so many full-text databases scattered around the Web that it can be frustrating to cover all the bases.

- **Searches what you type, not what you mean:** Full-text databases search for the characters in your search statement, not for the meaning of the words you type. In full-text databases, it is easy to have a search for the planet Mercury retrieve results as varied as "as the mercury soared to 102 degrees," or "the Mercury Cougar careened into the embankment," or "Mercury Morris will always be remembered," or "the mercury gray siding." Balancing specificity without too tightly narrowing your search is a skill developed over time.

- **Duplication of material:** Searching in newspaper files, for example, can retrieve multiple copies of the same article from different newspapers. Some newspapers even put in different editions' versions of the same story, often with little or very subtle changes.

- **Not comprehensive:** Do not assume that if something or someone is not retrieved in a search that there has been nothing written about them. Databases are a tool of inclusion (if you find it, you can assume it is there), *not* a tool of exclusion (if you don't find it, you can assume it isn't there).

- **Consider the source:** Errors in articles are not always caught. If a piece of information is important to the story you are writing, verify it with another source. To get the fullest sense of what your search has and has not revealed, you must understand how the articles and publications are written and how the database is compiled.

Finding full-text article and transcript databases

Commercial services
(All require a subscription—most are now searchable on the Web.)

- **BurrellesLuce**: *www.burrellesluce.com*
  Broadcast transcripts from more than 160 network and cable stations dating back to 1989. Not searchable on the Web.

- **Dialog**: *www.dialog.com*
  More than 90 U.S. and 40 non-U.S. newspapers. Full text to hundreds of specialty magazines. Searchable on the Web.

- **Factiva** (Dow Jones/*Wall St. Journal*): *www.factiva.com*
  Access to the *Wall St. Journal* and information from more than 9,000 news wires, business magazines, and major newspapers around the world. Searchable on the Web.

- **LexisNexis**: *www.lexisnexis.com*
  The mega-library of newspaper and magazine full-text sources. Massive legal resources databases. Searchable on the Web.

- **NewsBank**: *www.newsbank.com*
  In the past 25 years, Newsbank has gone from a microfiche-based clipping service to a full-fledged database vendor on the Web. More than 1,500 U.S. and international news sources.

- **Congressional Quarterly databases**: *www.cq.com*
  Legislative tracking and news service. Premier subscription service for non-partisan Congressional and U.S. political information.

- **Westlaw**: *www.westlaw.com*
  Legal resources databases. The subscription-based online version of Thomson West legal resources.

On the Web

- **NewsLibrary**: *www.newslibrary.com*
  A full-text database from 829 news sources that allows you to search for free but charges up to $2.95 to see the full text of each article you find.

- **Highbeam**: *www.highbeam.com*
  Search a free archive of more than 35 million documents from over 3,000 sources—a vast collection of articles from leading publications, updated daily, and going back as far as 20 years. Requires a membership to gain access to the full text of the articles you find.

- **FindArticles**: *www.findarticles.com*
  Claims to provide access to 10 million articles on a full range of topics. Allows you to search "free articles" or "all articles." Provides full text in either case.

- **Newsstand**: *www.newsstand.com* and
  Pressdisplay: *www.pressdisplay.com*
  Electronic reproductions of current editions of hundreds of newspapers from cover to cover.

- **Online Speech Bank**: *www.americanrhetoric.com/speechbank.htm*
  An index to and growing database of 5,000+ full text, audio and video (streaming) versions of public speeches, sermons, legal proceedings, lectures, debates, interviews, and other recorded media events.

Exercises

- Someone told you there was a great debate on "Meet the Press" last weekend. Find the transcript.

- Some kids at the local middle school got sick from something they ate in the cafeteria. You remember that happening a few years back to some school kids in Detroit, bad strawberries or something. See if you can find some background articles.

It is a very sad thing that nowadays there is so little useless information.
— Oscar Wilde

FOR MORE INFORMATION

Books:

Directory of Books and Periodicals Online. Vols. 1-5. New York: Library Technology Alliance, 2005. *www.booksandperiodicals.com* A directory of publications that can be researched electronically via online hosts, such as LexisNexis, Dialog, and Westlaw. It lists more than 146,000 sources including 87,000 journals and 57,120 full-text sources.

Glose, Mary B., Lara Fletcher, and Jennifer Fasolino. *Fulltext Sources Online.* Westport, CT: Information Today, 2006. *www.fso-online.com* A directory that lists nearly 30,000 periodicals, newspapers, newsletters, newswires, and TV or radio transcripts accessible online in full text, from 27 major aggregators. Published twice a year. It covers topics in science, technology, medicine, law, finance, business, industry, the popular press, and more.

BOOKS AND DIRECTORIES

Some of the most useful reference books are available in database form, and in that form are even more useful. Because every word in a database is indexed, information that is hidden or difficult to find using a traditional book index is revealed in a database search. Many of these useful reference works are also available on CD-ROM, a particularly cost effective method for searching frequently-used books.

Now that some of the best and most basic reference books are available on the Web, every reporter's desktop is a library.

Many of the publishers who made their directories and reference books available through a commercial database service now provide access through their own Web site. A good example of this is the Gale Group. While their excellent resources, like the *Encyclopedia of Associations* and the *Biography Master Index*, are still available on Dialog (*www.dialog.com*), you can also go to the Thomson/ Gale Group Web site (*www.gale.com*) and, if you have an account, search all their publications. Both are browser-based searches but one is through a vendor, the other through the publisher.

These kinds of shifts and options in the availability of basic resources make savvy shopping for information even more challenging.

Examples of book and directory databases

- **American Business Directory:** Information on more than 12 million U.S. businesses with information from press releases, annual reports, and other records. Produced by InfoUSA.

- **Encyclopedia of Associations:** More than 140,000 nonprofit membership organizations worldwide are profiled. Published by Thomson/Gale.

- **Complete Works of Shakespeare:** Shakespeare's complete works are searchable on this site from M.I.T.: *http://shakespeare.mit.edu.*

- **Books in Print:** Information on books currently in print from U.S. publishers, from R.R. Bowker.

- **Marquis Who's Who:** Detailed biographies of more than 790,000 individuals from the entire "family" of Who's Who print publications.

- **Martindale-Hubbell:** Legal directory of more than 1 million lawyers and law firms in 160 countries. More information at *www.martindale.com.*

- **Research Centers and Services Directory:** Information on more than 31,000 organizations conducting research worldwide. From Thompson/Gale.

- **Thomas Register of American Manufacturers:** Information on what is made, where it is made, and who makes it. Covers more than 174,000 U.S. and Canadian companies. More information at *www.thomasnet.com.*

Uses in reporting and research

- **Locate specific information:** Directory and reference book databases can help you track down people, quotes, companies, and obscure facts with only the sketchiest of information.

- **Find experts/sources:** Associations, foundations, and research centers are good places to contact experts in specific topics.

- **Get ideas about the scope of a topic:** Sometimes just browsing through names of associations and research centers can give you angles to a story.

- **Background and reality check:** Don't rely on what someone tells you; use a directory to find other sources who can verify their statements or fill in holes in their information.

- **Get "fun facts" and color:** Backgrounding something that happened on a certain date—what else happened on that date? Describing how big something is—what else is that big? Finding trivia and colorful details can add flavor to your story.

Advantages of book and directory databases

- Full-text indexing allows you to easily locate hidden information.

- These databases correspond to sometimes-expensive reference books; it may be cheaper to search as needed than it is to buy the book.

- The database version is usually updated with new information and corrections more quickly than the print version.

- Since this information is from well-organized reference sources, it is usually well-edited and reliable.

Disadvantages and cautions

- These are not necessarily comprehensive: Don't assume something does not exist just because it isn't found in a search.

- Some of the information in directories is from submission by the company or person (*American Business Directory*, *Who's Who*) so you must not assume that the information given is the unvarnished truth. Always consider the source of the information in book and directory searches, and any other kinds of research.

- The structure of many of these databases is fairly rigid. In order to do searches on particular fields or elements, you must understand how the database is compiled. Some fields require use of specific terms or else you will not get valid results. Use the sheets provided by the database vendor detailing the structure of individual files.

- Be careful when using Web-based reference books. Many of them are versions which are now in the public domain, but are extremely dated. *Roget's Thesaurus*, for example, is on the Web at *http://humanities.uchicago.edu/orgs/ARTFL/forms_unrest/ROGET.html* but it's the 1911 version. Obviously, this would be of little use in tracking contemporary terms.

- Some full-text versions of books on the Web have search functions so you can look for a term. Others are just the full-text on the screen, a long, long, long scroll of text. For those, use your *Edit/Find in Page* function on your browser to look for a word in the text.

Further cautions when looking at ready-reference books online

- **What is the source of the reference?** Is the reference an online version of a reputable reference source or is it a compilation by a hobbyist? In publicly-edited references such as Wikipedia, the quality and reliability of the entry will depend on the expertise of the contributor(s). Browser beware.

- **When was the reference last updated?** How current is the online version, is there a more current print version, or is there a more current version online somewhere else?

- **Can you get to it?** Some libraries are making reference works available on the Internet but may have copyright or license restrictions that allow only local or approved users access to the reference. Don't be frustrated by finding a great title in a search but being denied access to the resource.

- **How easy is it to get to?** If the connection to get to the Webster's dictionary is unreliable or slow and you use that dictionary all the time, figure out that it might be smarter to invest in a paper version of the reference book! Time is money, spend it well.

- **How easy is it to search?** Are you not finding information that you just know must be there? Be skeptical about the reliability of the search engine, and ask questions of the resource provider to make sure you are using the resource properly.

- **If it's not on the Internet that doesn't mean it doesn't exist**: Repeat after us: all the knowledge of the world is NOT on the Internet, all the knowledge of the world is NOT on the Internet. Don't think that if you can't find it on the Web there isn't anything on the topic. While Internet resources are growing quickly, there are billions of valuable reference books that are not, and probably never will be, available through Internet access. The Internet is a good source of supplementary information for some kinds of information searches. As valuable a resource as it is, it is not the be-all, end-all information tool.

With those cautions understood, let's look at some examples of ready-reference sources on the Internet.

Finding services with book and directory databases

Commercial services

- **Dialog**

- **Factiva**

- **LexisNexis**

On the Web

- **Internet Public Library: Reference Center**: *www.ipl.org/div/subject/browse/ref00.00.00*
  Links to great, reliable ready-reference resources on the Web organized by subject or by type of reference tool. Find almanacs, associations directories, biographies, calculators and conversion tools, calendars, dictionaries, encyclopedias, quotes, etc. All these resources are free.

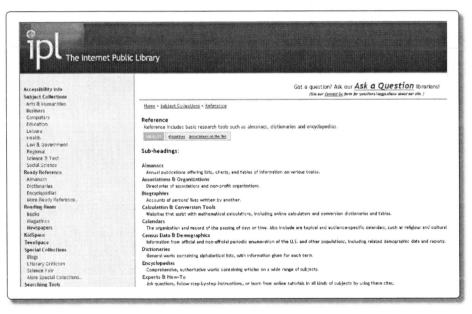

- **Research It!** *www.itools.com/research*
  This handy search site provides search boxes for information from encyclopedias, dictionaries, quotation finders, biographical directories, telephone area codes, etc. Love it!

- **Project Gutenberg:** *www.promo.net/pg*
  PG has been making electronic versions of classic books (those in the public domain) available for the past 25 years. Light literature (*Alice in Wonderland*), heavy literature (the Bible), and reference works (*Webster's Unabridged Dictionary*) are among the hundreds of available books. Find a title you want, download it to your computer, and run your own searches on it.

- **Google Book Search:** *http://books.google.com*
  The controversial but powerful tool that allows you to search the full text of current titles (not just those in the public domain). You initially get a "snippet view" which provides a few sentences of your search terms in context. If the publisher has given permission, you can see sample pages with the complete information. Otherwise, you are given a link to online bookstores that sell the title.

- **The Online Books Page:** *http://onlinebooks.library.upenn.edu*
  More than 25,000 free books are linked from this page. A great compilation service.

Exercises

- The flowery-speaking Speaker of the House, in a confrontation with a opponent on a bill, said, "Just as the King in *Love's Labour's Lost* said, 'Now step I forth to whip hypocrisy.'" You want to check if it really was the King in Shakespeare's play who said this.

- The seabird rescue mission director said, "If the pelican is worthy enough to be mentioned in the Bible, I think it is worthy enough to be protected…" Is the pelican mentioned in the Bible? Is it mentioned in every version of the Bible? Is the eagle mentioned? What about the robin? (Use this Bible browser—it has a great search template: *http://bible.oremus.org*.)

- You're fighting with your editor about using the term "disintermediation" in a story about a financier's activities back in the early 70s. He said that term wasn't even used then (and he sort of wants you to explain to him what exactly it means). Prove that the term was in use and find a definition.

- You're the government affairs columnist and decide to write your next column in rhyme. Find some good words that rhyme with "democratic."

GOVERNMENT DOCUMENTS

Access to government publications used to be one of the big selling points of commercial database access. The ability to quickly look up and retrieve presidential speeches, texts of legislation, and campaign contribution records was a tremendous aid to reporters. It came at a cost, however, causing a great deal of controversy over the need to pay to retrieve government information which your tax dollars helped collect.

The impact of the World Wide Web and its increasing use by government agencies to make official documents available is still being gauged by commercial database vendors. There had been attempts by the information industry lobby to close off the free access to some public documents (notably EDGAR, the electronic version of SEC documents) but they were unsuccessful and the number of government documents available on the Internet grows.

Read more about the information made available by government agencies in Chapter 3: World Wide Web.

Examples of government document databases

- **USA.gov:** *www.usa.gov*
  Gateway to millions of Web pages from federal and state governments, the District of Columbia, U.S. territories, and tribal governments. Much of this information is not available on commercial Web sites.

- **FedStats:** *www.fedstats.gov*
  Find statistics from more than 100 federal government agencies. Free.

- **Current Industry Reports**

- **Federal Register**

- **Patent Abstracts and Claims**

- **Securities and Exchange Commission Reports**

- **Weekly Compilation of Presidential Documents**

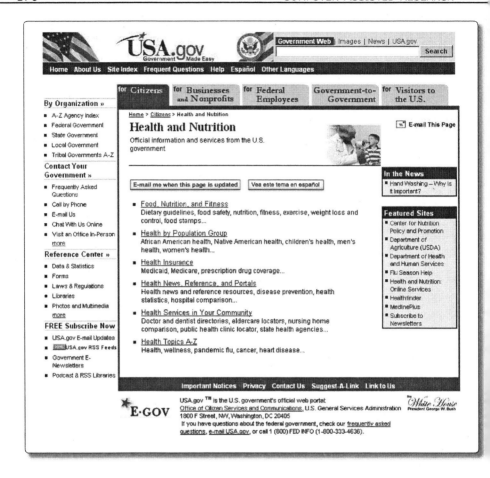

Uses in reporting and research

- **Find facts and statistics:** The U.S. government collects data and statistics on virtually every topic. These databases help make those figures accessible. You can even do searches on a figure (say, the national debt) and see if there are other items with that number that come up which might make an interesting comparison.

- **Reality check:** The capture of essentially every public word spoken by government officials, legislators, and executives means you can easily check back on what they've said in the past when you want to verify something they're saying now.

- **Background:** Financial information, congressional testimony, and other information can be used to help background people and companies you are writing about.

- **Finding experts:** Check in the transcripts of Congress to find names of people who have appeared as experts and testified.

Advantages of government document databases

While the disadvantage of a higher cost for access might weigh against the commercial vendor of government documents, there are some advantages to their use:

- **Information dates back farther:** Presidential speeches are available for free on the White House Web site (*www.whitehouse.gov*) but only for the current administration. The Presidential Documents database on LexisNexis dates back to 1979.

- **Accumulation of records:** Reports and studies sponsored by individual agencies may be sitting on their free Web site but you may have to go to a number of sites to do a search. Commercial database services can access compilations of these individual files, such as Dialog's access to National Technical Information Services' Bibliographic database. There are some government specific search services available on the Web now.

- **More targeted searching:** The commercial services take advantage of elaborate record structures to allow for field searching, which can help target and specify the types of documents you need. The documents available on free services often do not have field searching capabilities (although that is coming in some cases).

- **Faster:** Time is money, and sometimes connecting to those popular free government databases on the Internet can be time-costly exercises. When you need the information and you need it now, sometimes going to a commercial service is more efficient.

Disadvantages

- **Tracking down source documents:** Often, the information you retrieve is a reference to a government document, which you then have to locate to get the full text. This is particularly true for older documents.

- **Interpretation of data:** Statistics can be difficult to interpret; it is essential that you understand where the statistics come from and what they are based on. Use care as you compare statistics from one year to the next, making sure you are comparing like values.

Finding services with government documents

Commercial services

- **Dialog**

- **Factiva**

- **Newsbank**

- **LexisNexis**

- **Westlaw**

On the Web

- **U.S. Federal Government Agencies on the Web:**
  www.usa.gov/Agencies/Federal/All_Agencies/index.shtml

- **State and Local Government on the Net:**
  www.statelocalgov.net/index.cfm

- **Foreign Governments on the World Wide Web:**
  www.lib.umich.edu/govdocs/foreign.html

- **Legislative Information from the Library of Congress:**
  http://thomas.loc.gov

- **Political Resources on the Net:**
  www.politicalresources.net

PUBLIC RECORDS

Computer access to information about people is probably the most useful and most controversial area of computer-assisted research in newsrooms. Public records databases, from the simplest telephone look-up to more sophisticated dossier services, are invaluable to both deadline reporting and long-term investigations.

Information about people comes from three sources: records gathered by government agencies, information gathered by businesses, and content contributed by the person themselves. Think of them as records of one's life as a citizen, records of one's life as a consumer, and autobiographical information. We discuss the kinds of information that people contribute about themselves in the section on informal sources and social networking. Here we will talk about information that can be found through public records.

Public records from government agencies have always been available, but in paper form they were difficult or time-consuming to access. Information about consumers is a new area and probably the cause of most of the concerns about privacy. Each of these types of records has tremendous value in news research but requires extra care and knowledge when used.

Over the past decade many state and local government agencies have been moving towards electronic access to their records. While some of this information may be useful in issues stories (e.g. statistics on health care or water quality or road characteristics), we'll be talking here about databases that can help you track down people, their associates, their assets, and their personal histories.

The types of records, what they can provide, and what information you usually need to conduct a search can help you determine what information might help you get what you need. Some are state-wide databases, others are local compilations for which you would have to search county-by-county to get full coverage.

Examples of useful public records

- **Motor vehicle information:** automobile registrations, driver's licenses, accident reports
  - Can provide address, date of birth, driver history, social security number (in some states), physical characteristics of the driver (height, weight, race, sex, need for eyeglasses), and type of automobile driven (make, model, year).
  - Need to search by name (sometimes full name is required—sometimes date of birth is also required), driver's license number, VIN (vehicle identification number) or motor vehicle registration number.

- **Secretary of State filings:** incorporation records, uniform commercial code filing, limited partnerships
  - Can provide address information, names of business associates and associated businesses, name of company-registered agent, address of the business, status of the business, names of debtors and creditors.
  - Need to search by name of officer or business name.

- **Property records:** tax appraisals, mortgage filings
  - Can provide name and address of owner, characteristics of the house (square feet, number of rooms), mortgage holder and amount, appraised value, seller's name and date of sale, permits for improvements, liens on the property.
  - Need to search by address of the property, owner's or seller's name.

- **Utility records:** water and sewer billings
  - Can provide name and address of owner (useful for rented properties), delinquency of payment. (Check your water board members and see how they are doing with their bills!)
  - Need to search by property address, owner's name.

- **Voter registration records**
  - Can provide address information, party affiliation, last election in which they voted (but, no, you won't get information on how they voted).
  - Need to search by name.

- **Marriage/divorce records**
  - Can provide family name of bride, dates of marriage or divorce, record of previous marriages.
  - Need to search by name.

- **Occupational licenses**
  - Can provide information about business line, address.
  - Need to search by name.

- **Civil and criminal court cases/criminal history**
  - Can provide plaintiff and defendant names, lawyers' names, case file numbers (to get the full case record), arrest records.
  - Need to search by name, case number.

- **Other records of interest:** concealed weapons permits, boat and aircraft registrations, bankruptcy filings, mortgage default records, aircraft ownership, statewide criminal records.

Ways agencies make their databases available online

In addition to the regular telephone and mail-in request fulfillment services, many government agencies have been making public records available online through a variety of means.

Direct access to the agency's computer: An older and now less common means for access in the age of the Web.

- **Advantages:** The data are as current as the agency has available; you are searching the same database they use.

- **Disadvantages:** Sometimes the search interface is not designed for consumer use but for agency use and is not very user-friendly. It is possible the agency can monitor what is being searched on the database. Sometimes the database is available only during regular office hours.

Through a vendor: Public records resellers buy and repackage public records databases.

- **Advantages:** The interface for the database is more consumer-oriented and usually easier to use. There is often a wide range of databases available (by type of record or geographic area) providing "one-stop shopping" for public records. Some services pull records together, giving you a dossier of the person you are looking for. Usually, there is virtually 24-hour, seven-day-a-week access to the records.

- **Disadvantages:** Records are often not as current as direct access to the agency's database, so be sure you know when the records are updated. All counties in a state database may not be represented, so be sure you know the coverage of the data. You are paying a premium for the access and searchability of the data; it may be the more expensive access option.

On the Web: As with every other kind of information, public records are migrating to the Web.

- **Advantages:** *Free* for the initial search! Quick and easy search templates. Provides basic information (age, race, residence county, date of event, etc.).

- **Disadvantages:** Government agencies have figured out they can make a profit by providing free access for the search, then charging for the actual records in some cases.

Purchase the data and access on your own computer: Some news organizations purchase public records databases and store them on newsroom computers, allowing quick checks of names, addresses, salaries of employees, criminal records, etc.

- **Advantages:** No cost for searching after the data have been purchased. The data can run on software that is designed for easy use.

- **Disadvantages:** For databases with frequent updates and changes, the purchased database is quickly outdated.

Finding free public records from government agencies

- **BRB Publications, Inc:** *www.brbpub.com/pubrecsites.asp*
  This site has a "Free Resource Center" section that provides links to free government public record sites.

- **EDGAR:** *www.sec.gov/edgar.shtml*
  Securities and Exchange Commission filings for all companies, foreign and domestic. Company financial statements, annual reports, Forms 10-K, all other required periodic reports and much more are available in real time, along with a tutorial on using the database.

- **GuideStar:** *www.guidestar.org*
  A compilation of searchable data from IRS Forms 990 filed by the more than 1 million nonprofit organizations in the U.S. The database also includes the IRS Business Master File.

- **PeopleFinderNow:** *http://peoplefindernow.com*
  Includes lists of free search categories, most of which are based on public records.

- **PoliticalMoneyLine®:** *www.fecinfo.com*
  About 40 percent of the information from this comprehensive campaign finance and lobbying data database is free. Information is based on public filings with the Federal Election Commission, Congress, the Internal Revenue Service, and smaller agencies.

- **Searchsystems.net:** *www.searchsystems.net*
  This site provides free access to public records about businesses, corporate filings, criminal and civil court filings, vital records, property records, licenses, and more.

Vendors of public records

Many service companies are springing up which subscribe to the various public records databases and offer comprehensive search and retrieval of records in both electronic and paper form. Most of these services have a Web site.

Advantages of public records vendors

You don't have to have subscriptions to a number of different services. These services allow access to records in a number of forms through a network of searchers in various cities.

Disadvantages

Probably the most costly option since the search service passes along the cost of the search as well as a service charge. Quick turnaround service usually costs extra, and it may be several days before getting some records.

Examples of vendors of public records on the Web

This is by no means an endorsement of these particular services; they just provide an interesting inventory of the types of records available.

- **Accurint®:** *www.accurint.com*
  Widely used in news libraries, this is a LexisNexis service that provides one-stop shopping for public records.

- **AutoTrackXP:** *www.autotrack.com*
  Another common service found in news libraries, this is a ChoicePoint company that combines public records with consumer profile information.

- **PACER:** *http://pacer.psc.uscourts.gov*
  The Federal Judiciary's system provides access to case and docket information from Federal Appellate, District and Bankruptcy courts, and the U.S. Party/Case Index. The system eliminates the need to search the records of each federal jurisdiction separately.

Finding public records vendors

- Search the "Professional Vendor Locator" section of the BRB Publications, Inc. Web site: *www.brbpub.com*.

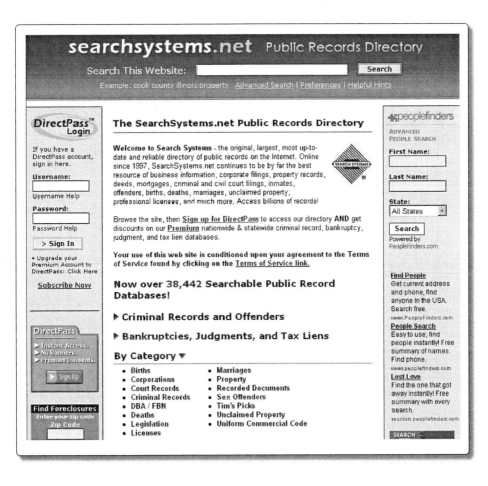

Finding public records databases

Not all states or local governments offer the same level of access to similar records. Not all records of the same type have the same information from state to state (for example, New York does not require the listing of officers names in the corporate filings). Although on the state level some public records search companies are getting more comprehensive access to records, the compilation of local level records is still highly variable. Here are some ways you can track down public records for your state and local area:

- **Check with the agency itself**:
  Determine which agency's files you would find useful for routine checks (corporate filings, drivers' records, and property records are generally the most useful). Call the agency's data manager and see whether you can arrange for direct access or even the purchase of files to load on your own computer.

- **Check with public records database vendors**:
  Several database vendors specialize in public records access. Shop around the different services to see which ones have the types of records you want and the most comprehensive coverage.

- **Check with your state press association**:
  Your state press association should be tracking public records access in your state. Several states have developed guides to public records.

- **Check with a university data center**:
  Many large universities have data centers with tape libraries of state data. They can tell you the status on the availability of different types of records.

- **Check with the state information center or the city/county data processing office**:
  These are the keepers of the information inventory. They will know what databases are available and the access there is to the records.

- **Do a Web search**:
  Genealogists are really using the Web as a way to share information about how to track down records about people. Do a search in one of the search sites for "birth certificates" or "death records" and you'll get all kinds of listings of places to call. Many will require some turn-around time, so don't think you can do this on deadline!

- **Check out the USGenWeb Archives**:

  www.rootsweb.com/~usgenweb

- **Look at Vital Records Information** (*www.vitalrec.com*) for a listing by state of where to get birth, death, marriage, and divorce records.

A critical step in locating public records is knowing your rights for access to the records. Again, your state press association or the Reporter's Committee for Freedom of the Press (*www.rcfp.org*) are good sources for information about records access.

CONSUMER RECORDS

Every time you change your address, subscribe to a magazine, get a telephone number, or apply for a credit card, you leave an electronic trail. So do the people you are looking for when you are reporting the news. Database vendors offer access to some of these databases which can be very useful in tracking down people or providing key pieces of biographical information. The access to records of different types can also help you verify, from a couple of different sources, information you have found.

In the past couple of years, information that had previously been available to researchers and reporters has been removed. For example, information from credit headers used to tell where the person worked. This is no longer available, except to those with permissible (under the Fair Credit Reporting Act, *www.ftc.gov/os/statutes/fcrajump.htm*) use of credit information (and reporters are not a category of "fair users"!).

But there are still useful compilations of data from consumer-based records such as:

- **Post Office change of address:** This information had previously been widely available, but now it is accessible on only a few services (WDIA's National Credit Information Network, for one). This has the change of address forms people fill out to have their mail forwarded to a new address.

- **People finders:** With just a person's name and the state he or she lives in, you can get a record of their address and telephone number. These databases are usually compiled from standard directories (such as telephone books) and other sources such as product response cards and magazine subscription cards.

- **Address search:** Nationwide criss-cross directories allow you to search on an address and get information on who lives there, telephone number, age of occupants (sometimes), and other residents. They usually have a feature allowing you to see the names of neighbors with their telephone numbers and addresses. Here's an example of the usefulness of neighbor access. When a plane crashed in North Carolina, an Associated Press reporter had the name of the church near the crash site. He looked up the address, got neighbors' listings, and started calling. The second number reached a woman who had had a burned survivor of the crash stumble onto her front porch just minutes earlier.

- **Phone search:** A compilation of listed telephone numbers. There are a number of phone search products and services. Be careful to determine which is the most current and most frequently updated, and which might include unlisted numbers. Unlisted numbers would be included if someone listed it on another source that is used in compiling the record—a magazine subscription form or credit application, for example. You won't get unlisted numbers from the telephone company and there is still no cell phone directory.

- **Credit headers:** A database of information extracted from credit reports. It does not include specific financial information but can provide you with current and previous addresses, social security number, month and year of birth, and spouse's name.

Finding people-finding services

On the Web there are lots of people-finder services with telephone and address search functions available. Which one is the best? Well, the one that has the name you are looking for in it! But that will be different for different people.

Someone from New York asked Nora which service she preferred and she ran his name and her name through a few of the services to show the difference in results:

- **Anywho** (*www.anywho.com*): Had him, didn't have her

- **Switchboard** (*www.switchboard.com*): Had her, didn't have him

- **WhoWhere** (*www.whowhere.com*): Had both, with most complete info

- **Yahoo! People** (*http://people.yahoo.com*): Had them both

As with all the search services, get to know a few well, but know where the others are in case your regular route of searching doesn't get you where you need to go.

Some other people-finding services to consider are:

- **Telephone Directories on the Web**: *www.infobel.com/teldir*
  The Internet's original and most detailed index of online phone books, with links to Yellow Pages, White Pages, business directories, e-mail addresses, and fax listings from all around the world.

- **PeopleSearch**: *http://peoplesearch.net*
  A meta-search site for people-finder databases. Put in a name and it will go out and do the search in multiple people-finder databases.

Examples of consumer records vendors

- **LexisNexis**: *www.lexisnexis.com*

- **MetroSearch**: *www.metrosearch.org*

Tips and traps in using public records and consumer records

As useful as these databases are in locating people you need to talk to, they are also the riskiest to use and potentially the most expensive. Keep these guidelines in mind:

- **Verify, verify, verify**: The old computer adage "Garbage In, Garbage Out" was never truer than with these databases. Usually this information is contributed by the person it is about (is anyone honest about their weight on driver's licenses?) and comes from handwritten forms which are keypunched into the database. Errors are rampant and it is essential that any information you find from these files be verified.

- **Consider the source:** Understand how the data came to be in the database, what is required of that particular record, and what kind of checking is done of the veracity of the information. Public records databases may be more reliable than consumer records, but someone with no car, property records, or utility bills may only be found in consumer records.

- **Get specifics:** If you only have the person's name and it is a common name, you might as well not search. Unless you have some specific information that can identify the entry as the person you are looking for, you cannot assume you have found the right person.

- **Don't expect miracles:** Some data are just not available. You can check the same name in different databases and just get the same information over and over. Know what you are searching. Also, privacy laws are getting stricter, so know what you can reasonably expect to find, and don't expect more.

- **Shop carefully:** Know what you are paying for and which database is being searched when you look at different vendors. You may be charged a premium for searching a database you could have gotten directly for much cheaper.

- **Don't forget the good old paper trail:** Lots of information is still not online. Much of the information that is online is just a reference to the full file which you'll need to get from the agency which created it. These sources are often good pointers to places to check, but they are not the whole picture. Remember, it's called computer-assisted research, not computer-complete research.

Exercises

- An accused bigamist named Charlie McGillis admits he married one woman in Colorado in the early '80s but he says he divorced her there a few years later. Find the marriage record and see if there was a divorce.

- Choose a major publicly-held company in your region and find the most recent financial statements filed with the federal government.

- The state Republican Party claims that faculty at the local university are "indoctrinating" students to support Democratic Party issues and candidates. Find out how many faculty at the university gave money to one or the other political party in the last federal election.

FOR MORE INFORMATION

Houston, Brant, Len Bruzzese, and Steve Weinberg. *The Investigative Reporter's Handbook: A Guide to Documents, Databases and Techniques.* 4th ed. New York: Bedford/St. Martin's, 2002.

Sankey, Michael L. *Public Records Online: The National Guide to Private & Government Online Sources of Public Records.* 5th ed. Lanham, MD: Facts on Demand, 2004.

MULTIMEDIA: PHOTOS, GRAPHICS, AUDIO, AND VIDEO

Pictures (still and moving) and sound, along with text, make up the multimedia Web page. Image databases with photos, charts, clip art, satellite images; audio collections of music, speeches, and news stories; and video files are now all available online. You can see company logos, patent drawings, photos taken by satellites, and drawings of the Starship Enterprise. You can hear speeches, catch that radio program you missed, and sample selections from a new CD. You can watch parts of yesterday's broadcast and "be there" at breaking news scenes.

Public libraries are making their historical photos available on the Web. Huge photo collections have sites that allow you to search and download images. Television news programs provide searchable archives. Just a few years ago the access to images and audio was limited to a few high-end commercial services, but now the seeker of multimedia content has a wide array of options.

After decades of text only archiving, the collections of multimedia content on the Web and through commercial vendors add a huge new dimension to the information marketplace.

Uses in reporting and research

- What kind of hat was Jackie wearing in the back of the limo when Kennedy was shot? A photo can tell you.

- When covering a candidate, don't just read his words (the written word conveys only a small portion of human communication): listen to his speeches to get more of a sense of his presentation and feeling.

- Get color, detail, and a sense of scene by watching video clips of news events.

Using multimedia databases

In order to see or listen to audio, video, and image files, you need certain plug-ins—add-on software for your browser. Usually if you go to a file and try to download it, it will pop up a box saying you need a particular plug-in, and then give you the option to go get it.

Finding image, sound, and video files

- **AccuNet/AP Multimedia Archive:** *http://ap.accuweather.com*
Search the AP's photographs, audio sound bites, graphics, and text spanning more than 160 years of history. Free to educational users; commercial users require a subscription.

- **Corbis:** *www.corbis.com*
Corbis, with more than 70 million images online, lets you find and download pictures. News organizations pay a licensing fee to use images from this database in their publications. This is a subscription service, but the company allows nonprofit organizations or advertising, design, and public relations agencies doing pro-bono projects to submit requests for waiver of the licensing fees for images used in their projects.

- **Footage.net:** *http://footage.net*
Allows global searches of hundreds of online footage databases worldwide. Includes records from stock, archival, and news footage collections. The search links you to the Web site of the collection where the materials can be found. Most link you to detailed descriptions of the contents with information on how to order the material itself. Requires registration.

- **Google Earth:** *http://earth.google.com*
Combines satellite imagery, aerial maps, and the power of the Google search engine to provide individual-address-level images from the entire planet. Most of the highest resolution images are from the U.S., but the database allows you to search for any location and find 3D terrain, buildings, local facts, and more, or you can just point to a particular location on the planet and the software zooms in. The basic version is free for download to any computer.

- **Google Image Search:** *http://images.google.com*
Claims to be the most comprehensive image search engine on the Web, with billions of images indexed and available for viewing. Some images may be protected by copyright so you need to contact the site owner for any image you find to obtain permission for use.

- **YouTube**: *www.youtube.com*

  YouTube started the phenomenon of easily uploaded videos on the Web, with everything from the sublime to the ridiculous. You can find segments from news programs, commercials and speeches. This is one of the places savvy reporters should search when someone finds themselves in the news — who knows, they may have uploaded a video of themselves.

- **Flickr**: *www.flickr.com*

  An example of a social networking site with a twist. People can create a profile about themselves and upload their photo collection. This is a great resource for finding esoteric images as well as possibly finding interesting people.

- **Library of Congress American Memory Project**:

  http://memory.loc.gov

  Free and open access through the Web to written and spoken words, sound recordings, still and moving images, prints, maps, and sheet music that document American history. Historical materials from the Library of Congress that have been digitized are the flagship project of the National Digital Library Program, which makes more than 5 million items available online.

- **Moving Image Collections**: *http://mic.imtc.gatech.edu*

  A collaboration of organizations of moving image archives that documents moving image collections around the world. Provides a searchable database of titles and another searchable database of repositories of moving images. Some moving image files are actually accessible on the Web, but most records lead you to the repository where you can request access to the images you need.

- **The Cartoon Bank**: *http://cartoonbank.com*

  A searchable database of cartoon humor from *The New Yorker* magazine, including individual single-panel cartoons and magazine covers from the 1920s until the present. All images are copyrighted and must be used with permission from The Cartoon Bank.

- **Internet Archive**: Moving Image Archive: *www.archive.org/details/movies*

  "This collection contains thousands of videos which range from classic full-length movies, to daily alternative news broadcasts, to user-uploaded videos of every genre." All immediately available for viewing.

Exercises

- Find a satellite image of your town.

- After a massive tornado destroys three-quarters of the town of Spencer, Iowa, you decide to do an historical piece about what the town had looked like over the decades. Find some images of Spencer.

- A huge water spout threw four fishing boats into the Skyway Bridge, and no one got any video! You want to add some water spout video to your Web page (noting, of course, that it is only an example of a water spout, it's not *the* water spout). Where can you find some images you could purchase?

A few words about copyright

Just because it's on the Web doesn't mean it's yours to use. Just because it's easy to do an image grab, doesn't mean you should. Check with the Web site that made the image available before you re-use it. Copyright issues are discussed in more detail in Chapter 5.

Chapter 5

Evaluating Information Online

Aside from knowing how to search efficiently,

one of the most frequently mentioned questions that journalists raise when asked about the Internet is, "How can I tell whether or not the information I find is reliable?"

It is somewhat puzzling that journalists, whose life's work is to scratch the surface of what they see and hear and get down to the truth, are so flummoxed by the delivery of information on the Web. They are trained BS detectors. They know how to go behind the spin and find the reality. They can look at the documents and listen to the glib statements and then ask the questions that reveal the whats, whys and hows.

So, why are so many reporters so stymied when they get in front of the computer screen? Why do they think the process of validation and verification of information on the Internet is any different than the process they employ every day in phone calls with sources, press releases, faxed documents, or stuff sent in the mail?

In this section we'll step through a couple of different approaches to thinking about Internet-delivered information. One comes from a journalist, the other from some librarians—representatives of two groups who base the credibility of their own work on their ability to judge the credibility of the information they use.

But before we start, a few words about information on the Internet:

- The Internet did not invent mis-information or disinformation.

- The Internet did not create rumor-mongering.

- The Internet did not spawn propaganda.

- The Internet is not responsible for dirty data and stupid statistics.

All of these types of content have been around forever; they just have a new distribution outlet.

The Internet *does* make it possible for mis-information, disinformation, rumor-mongering, dirty data, and stupid statistics to be distributed more quickly and widely than in the past. That's the bad news. But the good news is that there are more people looking at what is distributed on the Web and who will provide the voice of reason (good examples are the rumor-control Web sites where hoaxes and urban myths are debunked).

Think about it this way. Can you trust what people say in a newsgroup or a chat room? Could you trust what you heard in a bar, in a man-on-the-street interview, a PTA meeting, or from fans in the stands? The answer, of course, is no. The old adage of "If your mother says she loves you, check it out" predates the Internet but will serve you well here, too.

If you pull up a document on the Web and you can't tell where it came from, what would you do with it? Well, what would you do if you got a fax or a document in a manila envelope with no return address? Check it out.

If someone sends you e-mail and you don't know who they are, can you believe what they are telling you? If you get a phone call from someone you don't know, can you believe what they are telling you? It's your job to find out if you can believe what you read or hear, no matter what technology is used to deliver it.

Those criteria you used in the past to check out the document in the manila envelope, the overheard conversation, or the phoned-in tip will continue to apply as you evaluate the information you find on the Web.

Now, here are a couple of ways to think about the evaluation of information on the Web.

MIDIS

Steve Miller, *New York Times* assistant to the technology editor, came up with a hierarchical approach to judging Web site information. Modestly called "MIDIS: the Miller Internet Data Integrity Scale," this approach is a four-level scale for information found on the Web and how comfortable a journalist can be in using it.

Most reliable to use are:

• **Government data:** federal, state, and local
Miller says, "While you might personally question the data, you are safe in quoting from it (e.g. "...according to the National Transportation Safety Board...")."

Next are:

• **University studies:** peer-reviewed
Miller says, "Most studies by recognized experts in a field are still reviewed by peers. Quoting from these studies is also a safe bet with attribution."

Following that are:

• **Special interest groups:** an agenda doesn't mean the data are flawed
Miller says, "Even though we know that these groups have a political agenda, it does not follow that their data is flawed. It's also safe to use the data since it is attributable. "A study by Amnesty International claims that ... ."

And the least reliable, on the MIDIS hierarchy are:

• **Other:** Who is this person and why is he publishing this data?
Miller says: "This is information published on someone's homepage. Since anyone can put anything on a homepage it's a coin toss whether the data has any validity."

(Read a full description of Steve's MIDIS analysis at: *www.freedomforum.org/templates/document.asp?documentID=11642*)

The astute reader will recognize that Miller's categories mirror three of those we've been using throughout the book: our institutional sources are his government and special interest group sites, our scholarly sources are his university studies, and our informal sources are his "other" category of personal home pages.

Miller's hierarchy is fine if you want to know whether or not to use information that you then attribute to a source. But these days journalists need to know how to independently evaluate information, not just pass off other people's data with attribution. So how do you evaluate the actual quality of the information itself, not just the source to which you attribute?

That's where the next set of skills comes in handy.

AUTHORITY, ACCURACY, OBJECTIVITY, CURRENCY, COVERAGE

Journalists have the 5 Ws and the H (who, what, when, where, why, how) as a checklist of questions to answer when covering a story. Librarians, on the other hand, have the 2 As, 2 Cs and the O (authority, accuracy, objectivity, currency, coverage) as a checklist of questions to answer when evaluating information resources. The criteria that have been used to determine whether a book was a good one to add to a collection works well when judging the validity of information found on the Web.

Two librarians at Widener University, Jan Alexander and Marsha Ann Tate, have created practical guides to evaluating information found on different kinds of Web sites. Their site, "Evaluate Web Resources" (*www3.widener.edu/Academics/Libraries/Wolfgram_Memorial_Library/Evaluate_Web_Pages/659*), provides checklists for Web evaluation.

They have divided Web content into five different Web page types:

• **Advocacy**

• **Business/Marketing**

• **News**

• **Informational**

• **Personal**

For each type, they list questions you should ask about the page you are looking at. They say "The greater number of questions listed below answered "yes," the more likely it is you can determine whether the source is of high information quality." They even have some that are in bold which, they say, if you cannot answer yes to, why would you even *think* about using the information!

Authority: Can you tell who put the page together? Is it an "official" site? Is there contact information for the people who put the page together? Can you tell who wrote the material on the page and what their qualifications are?

Accuracy: Do they give the source for any "factual" information on the page so you can independently verify? Is the page well edited? (If they are shoddy with spelling and grammar, they may be shoddy with accuracy, too.)

Objectivity: Are biases clearly stated? Is advertising clearly differentiated from information content?

Currency: Can you tell when the page was written, posted to the Web, and updated?

Coverage: Is it clear what the page intends to address? Does it cover those areas well or are important issues left out?

Alexander and Tate's Web site is worth spending some time with.

Joe Barker, a librarian at the University of California Berkeley Library, has created another useful Web site that provides specific techniques to apply when evaluating information on Web sites. The page outlines the characteristics of URLs, identifies some of the indicators of quality information, describes how to find out what other Web pages link to the page you are evaluating, and more. His site is at *www.lib.berkeley.edu/TeachingLib/Guides/Internet/Evaluate.html*.

Exercises

Look over Alexander and Tate's and Barker's Web evaluation criteria and then take a look at the following. Which of these sites would you use? Why would or why would you not use them?

- You're looking for background information on biological warfare:

  www.emedicine.com/emerg/topic853.htm

  www.cbiac.apgea.army.mil

  www.brad.ac.uk/acad/sbtwc

- An Islamic school is opening in your town and you need to know more about Islamic education traditions:

  www.cie.org

  www.islamicedfoundation.com

  http://webpages.marshall.edu/~laher1/education.html

- You're looking for information about arthritis:

  www.arthritis.org

  www.pfizerch.com/brand.aspx?id=261

  www.niams.nih.gov

Tip

- Web search results often point you to a page deep within a Web site. Sometimes it's hard to tell who sponsors the page. You can go quickly to the home page (even if there aren't navigation aids on the page to get you there) by cutting back the long Web address to each previous element of the domain address (i.e. eventually getting back to www.xxx.com).

Tips

If you get to a Web site that does not identify who sponsors it or that does not give information about how to contact them, try finding the registration information from Internic's Whois service: *www.networksolutions.com/cgi-bin/whois*.

Or download the Alexa Toolbar (*www.alexa.com*) and use the "Site Information" feature to find who registered the site and get their address and telephone number. You'll want to contact them if you have questions, or want to find out if there is more recent information they have not yet loaded on the page.

Exercise

A link on a Web site takes you to the White House site: *www.whitehouse.net*. Hey, this isn't the White House site—it sure looks like it, but it isn't. So, who does own this site and what is its purpose?

Tip

It's amazing how many Web pages don't give you basic information like when the page was created. How are you supposed to tell how current the information is? Well, you can do a couple of things. Contact the Web master and ask (hopefully, they have e-mail contact information). If you are using Mozilla Firefox you can click on "Tools" on the browser bar and go down to "Page Info." It will tell you when the page was last updated. (But you won't know to what extent it was updated—maybe they just changed a comma to a period.)

Exercise

You are looking for information about how to get birth certificates in your state. You go to Vital Records (*www.vitalrec.com*) and find a link to information for your state. Go to your state's page. When was it last updated?

Tip

One of the best ways to get credible information is to go to credible places. Always think about where you would have gone off-line to get reliable information—then look to see if there is an online source to them. There are often copies of the same document sitting on different sites around the Web. Go to the originator of the information.

Everyone gets so much information all day long that they lose their common sense.
— Gertrude Stein

FOR MORE INFORMATION

Information Quality WWW Virtual Library
Written by Matthew T. Ciolek and Irena M. Goltz, these pages list online resources relevant for evaluation and development of online research.
www.ciolek.com/WWWVL-InfoQuality.html

Intute's Network's Virtual Training Suite
A set of free online tutorials designed to help researchers learn how to do effective searches and interpret the information you find for a wide variety of subject areas. Very clean, consistent template for every subject. Created by UK specialists but very valuable for everyone.
www.vts.rdn.ac.uk

NEWSROOM ISSUES WITH INTERNET USE

Despite the amazingly rapid adoption of the Internet as an information tool by individuals and workplaces, there are still newsrooms uncertain whether they want to make Internet access part of every reporter's desktop toolbox. There are others that have made access available but where the resource is not being used to its fullest potential. And in every newsroom that has the Internet there are concerns about managing the resources.

These are some of the concerns raised about Internet use in newsrooms and suggestions for what can be done about them.

The reporters will waste time.

- If reporters are wasting time because they don't know how to use it well, provide training.

- If they are wasting time because they don't know where good resources are, develop a news resources page or intranet.

- If they are wasting time because, well, they just like to waste time, go on a management retreat and figure out how to be better supervisors!

You can't trust what's on the Internet.

- Provide training about how to judge credibility of sites.

- Create news resource pages pointing to excellent sources of information.

They'll post stupid messages or download porn at work.

- Have a policy which defines the use of the Internet and e-mail at work.

They'll download a file with a virus and infect the network.

- Understand virus scanning and system security.

- Make sure your newsroom firewall is operating properly.

They'll take something from a Web site and use it in the paper and get us sued.

- Have a session on copyright issues and develop a policy for use of information found on Web sites.

There are so many subscription sites on the Web that we'll be wasting money if everyone signs on and then wants to get reimbursed.

- If you have a news research center (and you should), have it be the central clearinghouse of Web subscriptions and accounts. Provide information about the accounts and access on your intranet resource page.

Bottom line: with good training, clear policies, helpful guides, and sensible procedures, the issues the newsroom might have with using the Internet should be resolved.

TRAINING ISSUES

It always amazes us that huge capital budgets rarely have a line in them for training. This has certainly been the case with the shift to desktop access to the Internet. There's money for the hardware and the software, but none for the "wetware"—the people who will have to be using it.

There are many approaches to providing training on the Internet. Much of your approach depends on the current state of Internet usage in your newsroom, your goals for usage by the newsroom, and the resources you have available for training.

There is a tiered approach that many newsrooms take:

Evangelism: Initially, you're trying to drum up interest and enthusiasm about the Internet. Have large group sessions with demonstrations and talks by journalists from inside or outside the newsroom about how they have used the Internet in their work. Try to spread the word broadly about what the Internet is and how it can be useful, even essential, in reporting. The goal is to whet their appetite and get them to want to learn how to do it.

Technical: Hold training sessions on how to use to their fullest capabilities the technical aspects of the Internet (browser basics, how to use their e-mail system). These are often done in huge sweeps of the newsroom. The goal is to get everyone up to a certain level of functional knowledge of Internet software.

Departmental: Many newsroom training approaches next try to customize training to teach specific Internet and Web techniques to particular desks. What does the business desk need to use on the Internet? What would help the copy editors? How can feature writers take advantage of the Web? One of the goals here is to get a few people in those departments to become the point persons who can help others in the department when they have questions.

Individual: Ideally, training is ongoing and personalized. The most useful approach of all might be a twenty-minute session focusing on what an individual's daily information tasks are and pointing them to some techniques and resources to accomplish them. This kind of training will give that extra boost that will convince them of the Internet's usefulness to them and their work. And it will give them the confidence to explore further.

Who should do the training? If you have a news research center, the information professionals there would be the ideal trainers. That is certainly part of their training, to facilitate the use of information by people who need it. As we move to end-user information environments, the role of the news library will shift away from being a gatekeeper of the information to being a facilitator of its use and access.

If you don't have a news research center, designating a few Web-savvy (and enthusiastic) people in the newsroom can be a good approach. For the initial training stages, bringing in an outside consultant to provide mass training can be useful. But ultimately you'll be best served by developing an in-house network of experts and enthusiasts who can routinely pollinate the newsroom with Internet ideas and support.

Resources about training

- **NICAR**: *www.nicar.org*
  NICAR (the National Institute for Computer-Assisted Reporting) has an "on-the-road" training team which can organize a regional workshop or internal newsroom training. There are some great resources on their Web site for trainers.

- **IRE**: *www.ire.org/training*
  IRE (Investigative Reporters and Editors) has ongoing training in many aspects of reporting, with a central Web site for upcoming training opportunities around the country.

- **Computer-Assisted Reporting Bibliography**: *www.poynter.org/content/content_view.asp?id=1181*
  Written by David Sheddon for the Poynter Institute.

- **NewsU**: *www.newsu.org*
  The Poynter Institute's online training modules cover everything from writing tighter leads to improving your interviewing skills.

- **Council of National Journalism Organizations**: *www.journalismtraining.org*
  A journalism training site with a compilation of training opportunities for journalists offered by many different organizations around the country.

- **JournalismNet: The Investigative Guide to Internet Research:** *www.journalismnet.com*
  Canadian journalist Julian Sher has developed a resource page for journalists that includes a section on training resources (but check out the other things, too).

- **Bill Dedman's PowerReporting resources for journalists on training:** *http://powerreporting.com/category/Newsroom_training/Training_courses*
  An extensive list of training resources for journalists.

RESOURCE SHARING ISSUES

In the early days of the Web, when people found a great site they told someone else about it, maybe. Or they sometimes would exchange bookmark lists. But, for the most part, knowledge about good resources on the Web was held in little pockets all over the newsroom.

Then came the "intranet"—an internal site which uses the browser software and links to the Internet to make resources on the Web easy to catalog, organize, and search. In many newsrooms, the news library took the lead on developing these intranets. They quickly grew to include not just glorified bookmark lists but links to manuals and training guides, internal databases of information (personnel directories), access to acquired databases from outside agencies, and information helpful to employees of the organization.

Danish Broadcasting Corporation News Research manager Thomas Hedin created an intranet for his newsroom. "We have started with introducing our Intranet to the TV-news journalists," he said. "Most of them look like they have seen God." Intranets designed with a specific newsroom's needs in mind create a powerful portal to the Internet for their journalists.

The major advantage of the intranet is the ability to gather the collective intelligence of the newsroom. The best, and most vital, intranets are those which allow everyone in the newsroom to contribute good resources found along the way. In newsrooms which provide "in-house sabbaticals" (time on the job where the journalist's task is to go "play on the Internet"), part of the payback for "play-time" is the contributing sites they found for the intranet and a "brown bag" lunch training session.

There is an excellent resource page about newsroom intranets on the Special Libraries Association News Division Web site: *www.ibiblio.org/slanews/intranets*. The site includes background on building an intranet, links to several newsroom intranets as examples, links to the regular "Intranet Q&A" columns that appear in *News Library News*, and links to Web and SLA intranet resources.

Explore the use of del.icio.us (*http://del.icio.us*), a link sharing site, to create a universally accessible list of valuable resources (and check out the link lists of others who might have compiled interesting resources).

Having an effective, up-to-date, well-organized, and newsroom-tailored intranet may be one of the best ways to make the Internet effective and efficient for everyone in the newsroom.

FOR MORE INFORMATION

Intranets in News Libraries
Samples of a number of newsrooms' intranet sites. This site from the Special
Libraries Association News Division has a wealth of ideas.
www.ibiblio.org/slanews/intranets

COPYRIGHT ISSUES

We aren't copyright experts but even we know that just because something is on the Web doesn't mean it's yours to use however you wish. Browser software makes it so easy to grab a photo, copy and paste some text, or download a file, but that doesn't mean you should.

In fact, many Web sites do provide their information with the intention that it be freely used and distributed. They say so on their Web page. But they do expect to have any material used to be attributed to them.

Copyright on the Web can be kind of murky. For example, Corbis, the huge picture site, has a huge collection of free downloads for people to send as greeting cards or as computer screen savers, but then there is an even larger collection of photos for which they want a payment if you intend to use them.

ArtToday, a huge clipart site (*www.clipart.com*), offers a collection of more than 6 million royalty-free images, but you must pay a subscription fee to have access to the collection. Subscriptions range from $17.95 for one week of access to $169.95 for a full year of access.

Many news researchers express their concerns about the apparent copyright infringement routinely going on in their newsrooms. It seems there needs to be some consciousness-raising about what is and what isn't free to use on the Web.

Here are some resources about copyright and the Web. We strongly suggest that if your newsroom does not have a policy about copyright that is clearly communicated to the folks in the newsroom that they do so soon.

Copyright resources

- **American Library Association: Copyright**: *www.ala.org/ala/washoff/WOissues/copyrightb/copyright.htm*
  The Washington Office of the American Library Association provides a regularly-updated site that tracks copyright developments as they apply to libraries.

- **The Copyright Clearance Center**: *www.copyright.com*
  The Copyright Clearance Center provides guidance for businesses that face copyright issues.

- **Copyright Issues and Answers**: *www.poynter.org/column.asp?id=49&aid=1145*
  One of Poynter Library Director David Shedden's excellent bibliographies with many links to Web resources on the topic.

MANAGING WEB SUBSCRIPTIONS

Someone in your news organization is responsible for negotiating contracts for all of the resources that you and your colleagues use for gathering information. If you have a news research center, the news researchers manage subscriptions to print publications, CD-based tools, and expensive online services (LexisNexis, Accurint®, Autotrack) and manage the passwords required for all of these different services.

Those same people need to manage the subscriptions to Web resources. It is not feasible for everyone in the newsroom to have his or her own set of subscriptions to Internet sites that require a fee and password for access. Site licenses may be the answer for some materials. If journalists want to have access to subscription sites while traveling, that requires another round of negotiation. Each organization will develop its own strategies for managing Web subscriptions, but you *do* need a strategy.

The American Association of Law Libraries has a tip sheet that outlines strategies for negotiating Internet subscriptions at *www.aallnet.org/committee/criv/ resources/tools/negotiate.htm.*

ISSUES WITH INTERNET USE POLICIES

Tom Pellegrene Jr., Manager of News Technologies at *The Journal Gazette* in Fort Wayne, Indiana, wrote about the Internet use policy at their newspaper:

> "Basically, it says access to the Internet is company property much like notebooks and dictionaries are, so we are not to use our access for personal use...and we may not use the Internet to access sexually explicit material, even for an assignment, without the prior permission of the editor.

> This actually came into play a few months ago, when a local resident was charged with practicing medicine without a license when he castrated people (who volunteered) in his home. We needed to understand why people might do that and allow it to be done to them, and we thought that in addition to calling experts, the Internet might be helpful. The editor granted permission to a reporter to look around castration-related sites, but the permission was limited to that person and that story."

In other newsrooms, the Internet use policy covers how e-mail can be used, how to attribute information found on the Web, and other details of Internet usage.

A sample policy, written for the Associated Press, can be found at *http://powerreporting.com/rules.html*. This might give you some ideas of areas to cover in a policy. You might also talk with people on the online news staff about policy issues they might have (e.g. reporters answering e-mail from readers).

THE DISAPPEARING WEB

Keep in mind that the Internet information space is fluid and constantly changing. Don't assume that the report or the personal homepage or the magazine article you found useful in your research will still be there when you go back. If a Web page you've located is critical to your reporting, back it up by saving it with one of the site saving tools available. See "How to Save Web Pages and Web Sites for Offline Viewing" *http://tips.webdesign10.com/how-to-save-web-pages-and-web-sites-for-offline-viewing.*

IN CONCLUSION

The move to an Internet-connected newsroom is going to create some situations which, if not anticipated, will short-circuit all the best attempts at getting this resource available to the journalists and researchers who need it. Getting the newsroom wired is only a first step. The next steps will involve training, understanding, and managing this vast information resource that is now available.

KEEPING UP ON THE INTERNET

This guide has just been a kick start for using the Internet. There will be constant updates to Web sites and new techniques for research coming out all the time. Great new resources will be made available that you'll want to know about. How can you keep up with it all?

There are a number of techniques you can use to stay up to date with the Internet and Web resources.

Subscribe to listservs

- **CARR-L**: Computer Assisted Reporting and Research
  subscribe address: *listserv@ulkyvm.louisville.edu*

- **Newslib**: News Librarians Listserv
  subscribe address: *lyris@listserv.unc.edu or http://mail.unc.edu/lists*

- **IRE-L**: Investigative Reporters and Editors
  subscribe address: *listproc@lists.missouri.edu*

- **NICAR-L**: National Institute for Computer Assisted Reporting
  subscribe address: *listproc@lists.missouri.edu*

- **SPJ**: Society for Professional Journalists
  subscribe address: *listserv@lists.psu.edu*

- **Find beat-specific listservs at Google Groups**:
  http://groups.google.com

Keep up with changes in specific sites with e-mail alerts

- **ChangeDetect**: *www.changedetect.com*

Read magazines and newsletters

- **CNET News.Com**: *http://news.com.com*

- **Online**: *www.infotoday.com/online/default.shtml*

- **Searcher**: *www.infotoday.com/searcher*

- **CyberSkeptic's Guide to Internet Research**:
  www.cyberskeptic.com

- **Uplink/NICAR**: *www.ire.org/store/periodicals.html*

- **The IRE Journal**: *www.ire.org/store/periodicals.html*

Monitor "What's New" sites

- **Yahoo!**: *http://dir.yahoo.com/new*

- **"What's new"** on specific sites

Subscribe to the Scout Report

- Published every Friday on the Web and by e-mail. Helps readers stay informed of Internet resources: *http://scout.wisc.edu/Reports/ScoutReport/Current.*